God's Breath on Me

To Krissy

To Carole's baby Sister (who is my dearest friend)

God bless you

Tricia Banks

TRICIA BANKS

ISBN 978-1-68570-666-1 (paperback)
ISBN 978-1-68570-667-8 (digital)

Christian Faith Publishing
832 Park Avenue
Meadville, PA 16335
www.christianfaithpublishing.com

Printed in the United States of America

Father and Son

You are the smaller version of me
I speak my wisdom as you grow
So you will carry on my history
Commission studies you will know
Prophecy to those who need to be taught
Your knowledge acquired and forget it not
I pray you master each chosen skill
Through your life; I believe that you will
You are bound so close to me
My son, your eyes I hope will see
How I am training you to succeed
Not always follow but truly lead
Standing for what you believe
Setting goals you strive to achieve
A good and moral life; always to yourself be true
I prayed so many prayers for a son just like you
You are God's great miracle, my gift every day
I know you don't understand when you beg me to stay
But I am *always* with you; I was turned inside out
So pieces of my heart would always shroud you about
Shielding you, son, like armor; kept in sweet protective care
My love is a constant circle, holding you anywhere
I will dry your tears, my son; there is no need for you to cry
Know that I'm leaving with you though I blow a kiss goodbye
And watch my heart walk away from me, yet only to return
When you smile and wave so brave to me and quiet your concern
I know what you're thinking, for we don't constantly get our way
Through heartache and separation, we are restored another day

Refreshed in the arms of each other with stored-up memories
Savings in our heart banks; *I love you*s, and you *love me*s
Fonder are the hours while wrapped together in arms of love

Like a ribbon bound around us; bow-tied in our dreaming of
The strength to just get through and to lessen all this sorrow
I'll take your hand and pray you to a joyful tomorrow

The Second Commandment

Thou shalt not worship any graven image
Made by the hand of any man
Silver, gold, or wood; never could

See
For it has no eye
Hear
For it has no ear
Speak
For it has no voice
Think
For it has no mind or thought
Smell
For it has no nose
Feel
For it has no hand
Walk
For it has no feet
Love
For it has no heart

Those who make, trust, or worship them
Will become like the graven image made
When to any idol you have prayed

E
For *evil*

My Jesus
Is the Lord
He is real
He sees

He hears
He speaks
His Word
Is heard
He thinks
He knows
He shows
He cares
He smells
He feels
He touches
He heals
He walks
He loves
He listens
He forgives
He lives
He saves
He came to earth to die for us on the cross
His love for us paid the price; death was the cost
His love is true; forevermore given unto you

L
For *love*

A Better You

Smile
It is a pleasant greeting without a word
That brightens your face and someone's day

Pray
Ask and you shall receive
Give thanks for the blessings that come your way

Labor
Do a job well done
Intended for the One
Not for man but for the Lord

Be giving
Provide for the poor what they can't afford
Be humble, expecting no reward

Keep self-control
Hold your temper; don't raise your voice
Be disciplined; you have that choice
Not giving in to the devil's schemes
Maturity contained by all means

Bless others
It returns tenfold
To the young and old

Love
One another
Honor
Dad and mother

Be thankful
In all things; good or bad
Whether happy or sad
Grateful for each lesson that makes us grow
Life is a gifted journey, even though
We will have losses, but stay in your praise
Greater is the gain in our thankful days

Be kind
In your words and deeds
It plants sunshine seeds
Kindness always leads
To a blessed heart
It shreds hate apart

Be faithful
Expect what is unseen
For it is eternal
On the Lord; learn to lean

Be still
Find time to rest
With thoughts expressed
To the Lord and Savior
Quieted by His favor
Ceased is my striving
With God reviving

Be gentle
Touch another soul
Allow God His control
Used by Him to console

Be joyful
Embrace your joy like a friend
Sweet delight will never end

Holding hands, sharing treasure
Happy thoughts bring us pleasure

Trust
The only judgment I can find true
Is always constant; my Lord in You
On You alone, I can rely
Perfection cannot tell a lie

Use your gifts
We all have talents; God is gracious in His giving
Uniquely created for our purpose-filled living
Meant to share that He be glorified
Shining like a light, you cannot hide

Be confident
Only in the Lord, not your own understanding
Secure in His Word and His arms of safe landing

Be content
Satisfaction is found in all grateful hearts
Count your blessings as every morning starts

Have no fear
Only fear the Lord, for you were not given a spirit of fear
He has overcome the world and not all things are as they appear
I'm sheltered under His wing
My Lord can do anything

Just believe
Because it is true
He created you
To enjoy and to be blessed
In His arms, you will find rest

Keep hope
It is the anchor of our security
When we stay hopeful in our expectancy
Unmoved by doubt until the result we see
Granted by His mercy and His grace
He transports us to our hope-filled place
He changes who we are when satisfied
Growing in trust we kept anchored inside

Forgive
Often this is so difficult to do
When someone has broken the heart of you
Hurting your child in an abusive way
Your human heart wants them to dearly pay
You suffer with them in their pain
It's natural that you refrain
By forgiving them, you let go
Their power that still hurts you so
Forgive and leave it a God matter today
You will find peace as the pain melts away

Be strong
Only in the Lord
For you can do nothing without His strength and mercy
Greater by the Cord
Entwined with the Spirit; empowered you shall be
A conqueror in the battle of your enemy
Falling at your feet as you stay strong in the Lord
Armored like a soldier, marching long and forward

Share good humor
Cause someone to laugh, flavored with comedy
Just say something funny, but do it nicely
Nothing to demean to hurt other's feelings
Laughter paints all faces with such great healings
It boosts the bodies' immune efficiency

Lifting spirits as well as healthier you'll be
Shine on to a better you
Share His light in what you do

Be humble
That you may be exalted
In your future days
Never boastful nor arrogant
In your ways
Meekness is not a weakness
Showing strength in quietness

Addiction

Take this sin for I am weak; it has me chained
I find myself fatigued, with a weeping soul
By my own strength, there is nothing gained
Without You, I'm nothing; with You, I'm made whole

I know I must change this behavior in me
I'm too stubborn in my will to let it go
Knowing there is no excuse, You'll see
A valid reason for the sin I already know

Addiction to anything is like a prisoner kept
In a cage with a demon you've not conquered yet
The guilt gets to you, but then after I've wept
I light up again and nowhere do I get

Satan is the lie much like the smoke I inhale
The temple of body now fatigued and unwell
Addiction will always be a sad story to tell

I *can* do all things through You, Lord
These cigarettes I can't afford
But I keep smoking when I'm stressed
I know it's wrong (as I've confessed)

Take this sin, for I am weak; it has me chained
By my own strength, there is nothing gained

All of You

Perfect in wisdom, mind, and way
Sinless with holy completeness
Ever strong, never a weakness

Master of All; always in control
Most Faithful Friend who will console
Never will leave you standing there
Anxious to meet you anywhere

His shoulders are great as a mountain
Holding the care of the world
Sword of the Spirit is His fountain
Living and flowing, "the Word of God"
Verses written and unflawed
Instruct the path of life hard trod

No wealthier Gift-Giver will you find
The Richest Teacher, no other so kind
Talents granted that blow your mind
Favored on "His chosen" by grace
Betoken any age, of any race
All equal in His sight
This world can't get it right
We brothers and sisters fight

We all have His DNA
It doesn't matter what you do
Or believe in what you say
We *all* have purpose each day

He alone makes something out of nothing
He'll take a nobody and make him a king
Give voice to the dumb; power to sing
Deaf to hear angelic praise
Blind to see the light of days
Crippled legs stand strong and healed
Dead brought to life; heart sealed

All of You is perfect in every way
You never change, the same You stay

I am weak, but through You, I am made strong
My weakness shows me I need You all my life long
Teach me to trust in You every breath of each day
In everything may I learn, yielding to Your way

Always with You

Constant is His presence, near us every day
Commanding His angels to guard us on our way
Wherever we go, Spirit opens eyes to see
How Father cares and guides us where we need to be

In various ways, He reveals His loving care
The Keeper of all promises; He is always there
He'll greet you in the morning by a spirited prayer

His face shines upon you like the setting of the sun
Wrapped in the warmth of Him as the day has just begun
You are filled with His peace, knowing you're a chosen one

When opening your mind to receive His holy thought
You let go the sin of another that you have fought
Releasing the rope that had you tied up in a knot

Within me, there is so much change that needs to take place
But He is always with me, constant in His grace
As I am in a hurry and running my own race
To accomplish tasks I've started and wait until I'm done
To breathe You in and let you control them one by one
Unimportant may be the task, but I did not wait
For Your thoughts within me, then it is too late
Forgotten is what matters, and I make my mistakes
Angered at myself for creating my own heartaches
Forgive me for all the time I have wasted away
I truly need You with me every single day
Spirit, guide me in my deeds and the words that I say

The Evening of April 19, 2016

Today, I thought I would sit down and write. I had been spending many days and endless hours compiling my manuscript. I looked at the clock and realized I have sat for six or seven hours. I would not eat, sleep, or seem to be aware of much going on around me. I was transported to another place and time as I write. The words flowed, cascading like a waterfall. If I would not record them on paper or type them up, I couldn't retain them. It is a gift. I could not do it without the hand of God.

Today; He had other plans for me. I was to get in my car and drive. I went to the store then started to head south. I was directed to turn around and take Highway 92 east. I stopped in Bevington, which is east of Patterson, Iowa. I went into the "Hitchin Post" to eat a sandwich. I had not eaten all day. It was so delicious, but there was a platter full! I could not finish it. Leandra was my waitress, and I was very impressed with her great service and warm smile. Everyone was so nice and friendly. I felt so relaxed and comfortable, feeling of being home with friends surrounding me. I had never been there before. I will go again for sure.

I left after paying and drove west toward Winterset. On the edge of town at Cedar Bridge Road, I said out loud, "Oh, what a beautiful sky!" I was prompted to take a picture immediately. And so I did without questioning. I thought I snapped two. There were many trucks and cars heading eastbound on the highway. I quickly placed my iPhone down on the passenger side seat beside me. It was shortly after 6:30 p.m. It was a time of heavy traffic, so I had been very careful, but I felt reassured with someone else taking the wheel for that brief moment.

I got home and went to my photo album menu on my iPhone. I was surprised to see six cloud formations captured. What I saw with my human eyes while driving was totally different. Awed and in humbled disbelief, I counted angels. Each time I picked it back up and searched the clouds, I found more revealed. Others saw what I had not seen yet. I shared it with my son, Kevin. I was so excited.

It was the following day I realized that all the oncoming traffic that was headed eastbound was not in any of the photos! How could they not have been there driving toward me? That highway lane was clear in all the pictures. How did they vanish? I did not understand. It's a God thing, I know.

Turning my phone sideways and straight on, I found angels, arms locked together; Jesus; and a large dove with open wings. Our God is an amazing God of grace, miracles, and love.

April's Rain

Family clouds shout their joyous cry
All joining hands in the wide-open sky
So close to heaven, sharing with earth
Spring drink of life to induce rebirth

Piano keyed down the windowpane
Running down spout like a flowing vein
I inhale the fresh perfume of April's rain

Thundering drums the soil awake
And ends her nap through winter break
Mother trees bathe in cleansing showers
Young buds nurse for growing powers
Grasses gently kiss in a slow dance
Dipping for a much greener romance
Flowers peekaboo at you
Spring fashioned, bright and new

Family clouds shout in thunder
Standing renewed while I'm under
Baptizing raindrops, veiled and crowned
Soul caressed by drum rolling sound
In cleansing and quenching His handmade earth
She yields to Father in virtuous rebirth

Atoning Sacrifice

My precious Savior and Lord
Bore my sin; pierced by the sword
On the cross, His blood was poured
His crown of thorns had deeply cored
Wounds that bled
From His head
Day turned black while all clouds roared
To the Father, His cries soared
Knowing His death brought forward
The atoning sacrifice
Through the blood of Jesus Christ
All sins on His body were shored
His shed blood still flows toward
From that darkened day it first poured
To future by the risen Lord

Beautiful Markings

I've earned through blessings each line
Through childbearing because they're mine
Gifted with the proof on my lower abdomen
With each child, brighter ones began
Stretching out to give each baby room
Anxious to see them leaving my womb
Home is brighter with the child you bear
Happy lines by laughter, drawn here and there
Crow's feet are stamped through your worry
When late getting home, you're left in a scurry
Walking the floor until they walk through your door
Frown lines on your forehead are from intense thought
Double thinking for child and self, forgetting not
To you, your child has only been lent
Not belonging to you, yet still heartened
A mother's deepest marking
Is when her child is taken
When losing a child and their life has ended
Missing them so will tear her apart
Changing who you are
The saddest markings on her heart
Time has a way of healing
But signs are revealing
Shown on mother's face
Blessed, God-given grace

To bear a child makes you a mother
Compared not to any other-
Kind of fulfillment and love
Beautiful markings she's made up of
Dark circles under each eye
Lack of beauty sleep is why

Cradling the nursing baby
Or the teen years, maybe?
Yes, for certain; oh my!
Just the thought can make you cry
Then comes the empty nest
When you watched them fly
Away from you, thought I'd die
It feels like mourning a loss
(Losing what was never yours anyway)
Their lives get busy; you get to cross
Plans get changed to some other future day
You awaken from a dream you just had
Of your child so small once more
With tears streaming, it makes you feel sad
If only little feet would run through the door
Age spots are holy kisses I have found
Because I'm alive in joy, above ground

Being a Mother

It changes what you are when you birth your first child. You become a mother then. I never knew the nature of a mother's love until I looked upon the face of my newborn for the very first time. You share your first cries: the newborn cry and the new mother cry. I was aware of angels in the delivery room. I knew God was there too.

I felt a deep warmhearted euphoria flowing through me, my baby, the Creator, and began to breathe in the holiness of sacred company.

This kind of love-joy occurs for me only through the birthing of my children. Every child is a gift. Mine are. Not one is ever a mistake. God lends them to us. They belong to Him.

Home is transformed when you return. It is now full of living colors: sunny, much brighter, warmer, and sweeter. There is a satisfying fulfillment you've never felt before. You weep with a glowing smile when you hear the music of their fresh songs. Little squeaks when stretching, heavenly coos when talking, and looking at you because they know who you are. The hungry cry begs to nurse from the heart of you, remembering that drumbeat while in your womb. You melt in the beautiful sonnets of being a mother; loved and needed.

A God-given diploma constitutes mom as a teacher. Her child's world becomes her classroom of instruction and guidance. Mothers teach values and spiritual lessons. Home is the first church they learn to pray in. She becomes a double thinker; one thought for her child and the second for herself. I truly believe a mother's prayers are favored with precedence.

Your body has changed, with arms transposed to a gentler holding. Mother's eyes are more alert. Her heart will leave her body. She'll grasp it in her hand when the child takes hold of hers. You watch your heart walk outside your body when they take those first steps into your arms. They may fall; you always fall in love with them over and over again. The heart out-of-body experience happens the rest of your life. It continues with being a grandmother and great-grandmother.

When they grow to adulthood, you are still never alone. They never leave you. Still fastened to mother with a heart cord. The doctor cuts the umbilical cord, but you are forever connected. You are permanently bonded to each child, their children, and all the many people who touch their lives. Even death cannot cut the cord that connects mother and child. Death does not end our relationships.

Believe in Me

Peace, be still
Reach, I will
To take your hand
Now understand
I am for you
See what I do

I bless you every day
Bringing hope while on your way
Trials may come to test
Believe in Me for rest
I will place angels on your path
Fight your enemy with My wrath

Give you strength in all that you do
Create endurance, see you through
And in My arms, I'll carry you

Keep hope as an anchor, My child
Though many storms of life rage wild
I am there right by your side
I know the fear you cannot hide
Your thought I know unspoken
Your heart when it is broken

I am with you, come what may
Shine on you to light the day
Those dark hours fade away

I'll not leave you anywhere
Speak My name, and I'll be there
Sheltered under the wing with care

For I love you
With an everlasting love
And I can do
More than your heart could dream of

Just believe
And receive
Peace, be still
Reach, I will
To take your hand
Now understand
How I love you
See what I do

Isaiah 41:10

Be Still

Be still and know
In waiting we grow

Be at rest and trust
Your thoughts He'll adjust

Be quiet, and the truth is revealed
Spend time with HIM; your mind is healed

Be still and know
By faith, we show
In HIM we trust;
Alone we must

In quietness, HE shares HIS thought
Found is the wisdom I sought
Crowning me like a cleansing rain
Alone time with HIM, I gain
Strength for endurance
Loving reassurance
Guidance through the day
Protected I will stay

Be still and know
In waiting we grow
And our faith will show

Blessing of Pain

It is a blessing
You may not agree
To feel pain reminds me

I am alive, and I can feel
To a paralyzed one, it would be real
No longer numb from waist down
Able to move and dance around

Prompts you to go to the doctor and find
Why in pain and ease your mind
It is arthritis, but you'll live
Oh, the blessings pain can give

Losing a loved one, that leaves you sore
It's an ache that stabs you to your core
But with each loss, there is a gain
Rainbowed and tied after the rain
Still connected eternally
The sun fades out your misery

It creates endurance with a will that's stronger
By prayer, you go further and stand longer

I see, I feel, I speak, and I am not weak
Through my pain, I have grown
And by others, I have known

Blessings

Wake up and smile
And count awhile
Your blessings that are all around
How many can you write down?
Start with this very day
If things don't go your way
Remember that faith is your test
Strengthening you to be your best
Building endurance through resistance
Like our many trials for instance
We learn, and we come to know
By His tender mercy, we grow
He'll never leave you; He loves you so
Your hand is held by His strong right
So don't let go; give up the fight
To take control and do your will
Forgetting His; you can't be still
So you think you can do better yet?
Who sees your needs are always met?
He is in control; all power comes from the Lord
To give you *all* the blessings that you can't afford
We take so much for granted; we really do
Who breathes every breath of life into you?
You can do nothing beyond what He has planned
Hold His outstretched hand; He'll help you understand
Blessings are bestowed to you every day
Bright morning star does shine to light your way
Guiding you to treasures you often miss
Wake up and smile, remember this
Lift your head high, don't put it down
Slow your pace and just turn around
See blessings wherever you go

Share them with those you don't know
Bring smiles to a stranger's face
You can make friends any place
Blessings will never end
When you find a true friend

Brandon's Song

Mild as a summer breeze
A soft voice whispered,
"Rise, be with ease
Wake thy soul and follow me."
Hushed was I as she waved her hand
Less than a second of *our* time
We were in the Promised Land
I went groundward on my knees
Kneeling on a path of gold
Lined with many crystal trees
Like the wintered tree with ice
But not as stunning as these
Constructed perfectly nice
The loveliest of voices choired in harmony
Not *heard* of ear, yet found of me
Waves of hymns like fingers
Piano played in my heart
Caressing as it lingers
Breathtaking floral gardens were landscaped there
What a sight of glorious color and beauty
All touched with His most magnificent care
The eyes of my soul cannot close
My thoughts are oh-so clear
The angel holds a pure white rose
And bends close to my ear
With gentle breath, she speaks his name
I turn, on the note of *his* voice
I see my son; he looks the same
She spoke to him in spirit
He smiled such a brilliant smile
I swear that I could *hear* it
He did not see me, I believe

The angel bent again to me
She said, "No *more should you grieve*
He's safely home for eternity
Waiting for you, his sisters and brothers
His crown is jeweled; more than some others

You will see his jeweled crown one day
You must now go back. I will lead the way"
As we turned to go, he began to sing
And I will remember every word
"Home of the saints, our *day spring*
Home of the saved, our *shepherd*
Home of the table of honor and grace
Where our prayers of thanksgiving we share
Where *Father of Love* builds you a place
He knows you will be happiest there
Home, our joyful paradise
Where hearts are pure at the door
Standing clean, sinful no more
Master, Savior, here we are
You are the Bright Morning Star
Light of the World and the Lamb
The Lamb of God, the Great I Am
You brought me *home* to be with You
You love me so; I love You too"

Why he sang alone I did not know
And I felt my spirit just overflow
The choired voices did not sing along
Angel whispered, "It's Brandon's song"
I took one last look upon his face
Before I left that enchanting place
Truth followed me and held my hand
Thank you, angel, I understand
Love was always in the Master's plan

Brayden Tyler

My arms ached to hold you
And never let go
Watching you in NICU
I just did not know
How my heart could beat
And I could see
It beating in you
And outside of me

I feel the breath of heaven's love
As I hold Brayden close to me
God sent the son I dreamed of
He cries; for my face, he cannot see
So I lay him gently between each knee

My son searches my face, and he hears
Words from my heart, and I start the tears
Love brought you to me, my precious son
You couldn't be more perfect, beautiful one
He knows my voice, my scent, and my care
I promise you, Brayden, I'll always be there

Hugs and kisses
With heart's wishes
Love, Daddy

A Captured Bird

She walks the floor with heavy arms
Inside her head, a clock alarms
Ticking away, can't shut it off now
She wants to leave but doesn't know how

He bruises her with words of shame
His drunken self he'd never blame
He calls her another woman's name
Unfaithful husband is truly wicked
With all that pain he has inflicted

Returning home so late at night
He wreaks on sin and starts a fight
She can't stand that putrid smell
The raging drunk, she knows full well
Has planned another night of hell
Knuckled fists land on her head
Each knot is big, so sore and red
And pushes her hard to the floor
She can't take it anymore

Picking her up, he slams her to the wall
Dazed and weak, quick is her fall
He deplores, "You're not hurt at all"

Her thoughts are only on one
The trauma to her unborn son
He throws her over his shoulder
Implanting a stomach boulder
Then tumbles her helpless onto their bed
She quiets her cries through pillowed head

Hoping her two children won't hear
Sleeping and not awake in fear

He holds her prison, no way to leave
For her children, she does grieve
Like captured birds locked in a cage
She's black-and-blue during his rage
So afraid, nowhere to turn
Embarrassed but then she'll learn

To her pastor, she chose to confide
Then to the doctor, who with her cried
He stood there right by her side
Knowing what made her bleed
And ordered her the saving need
To leave before she lost the baby
You must leave this man who's crazy
In that small room, he placed a call
His lawyer friend would start it all

God would not have you live that way
The fear in you pressed you to stay
But what about the one who can't speak
An unborn babe or child to meek
Who also has been bruised
Watching momma so abused

A captured bird, I learned to fly
Away from him and did not cry
I spread my wings toward a sunny sky
Didn't look back or ask him why

Casting Stones

Don't spend precious time and don't you worry
When jealous minds and hands are in a hurry
To throw their stones in evil madness
They want your joy; they live in sadness
Wanting and hoping to be more like you
Don't give your power in the evil they do
Be true to yourself and do be kind
Forgiving them for their state of mind

Love the person, just hate the sin
Hating the person, you won't win
Ignorance you may find so vile
But you must humble yourself awhile

Pray and care for that lost soul who bleeds
For they see in you what their heart needs
Don't let them hurt you by words said
Remember that their soul is dead

They do not see yet with the Lord's eyes
Yours are open, not devil disguised
Salvation will be their new sight
God will bring their evil to light

Your breastplate is your godly shield
To casting stones, you will not yield
Surrender not to lies and blame
Cover evil in Jesus's name
Praying joy in place of hate
While the evil lies in wait
To cast a stone in your pathway
Or try to knock you down today

Chain of Blessings

String a pearled necklace
With never-ending links
Add diamonds to your chain
Use all blessings you attain

Collect your jewels daily
They are found everywhere
God spreads them with loving care

You'll find them when you're lost
When eyes are blurred with tears
I've gathered many gems through the years

Glittered stars brightly shining down
Cascade a row of emeralds found
Lighting up in a fiery sound

Blessings flow; acknowledge them
Be grateful for each new gem

Cradling Brandon

I cradled you, my son, in a bentwood rocking chair
I find the sweet memory of nursing you there
Singing you a lullaby or humming a soft tune
I knew that you and I would be falling asleep soon
Trying to stay awake, I kiss your face with my smile
Then we dream of the angels who visit us awhile
They tell you they miss you; the song of your laughter
You are my sweet blessing; they help look after
You left heaven to come to me
My sunshine boy is so happy
I love it when you awaken
It is then that I am taken
Into your raptured world of joy
Sunny bright with my baby boy
In my heart, you lit a candle star
And for always that is where you are
The radiance of your smile inside
Glows in my heart with beloved pride
I squeeze you gently with loving care
Cradling you in our bentwood chair

Creator of All

He gave a name to every star
And remembers what they are
That's why they shine so brightly
Playing Him a melody

He made birds to fly
They know Him; that's why
They soar in His sky
Reaching upward
Close to their Lord

The fruited trees where they can rest
Give food and shelter as they nest
His eye is on the sparrow, He cares for
And all the children which He loves more

Mountains quiver with pleasure
Kissed with dew droplet treasure

Flowers wave to say hello
Because the Maker, they know
Stretching in the sun's glow

Waters rise to praise His name
Each body commends the same
Whether ocean or great sea
Applauding tides sound for Thee

God spoke the day, "Let there be light"
And separated darkness for night
Painting a moon of mystery
Enthralled by it through history

Our God created every beast
Then planted a garden toward the east
In Eden, He placed Adam there
Eve, He molded with potter's care
God caused upon the man to sleep
To take a rib as he slept deep
And from man's rib, He created Eve
United as one to his wife shall cleave

Creator of all heaven and earth
Giver of life; His breath of rebirth
His miracles in abundance be
He'll open your eyes so you can see

Dare to Dream

You can make your dreams come true
Envision it granted to you
Let it burn within you like a fire
Do not let your dreaming retire
Give it passion like a breathless kiss
Let nothing stop you, remember this
Work your plan, brainstorm it through
Even baby steps bring it closer to you
Progress is made never letting it go
Share dreams with friends you know
Insight is found in the strangest places
Magic is made in helpful hands and faces
That smile and nod, with a pat on your back
Ignore those who try to throw you off track
They wish to be where you are in your dream
Closer to your goal with a supportive team
You're a miracle worker; power within your core
Faith will lead you; they will be dreams no more
They'll be fruitful, born from God's own will
Keep believing in its reach until
It all falls into place
Granted by His grace
It is worth the time and pain
The many dreams one can attain
When nothing stops you, remember this
When fired with passion like a breathless kiss

Daughter and Mother

Too busy to take the time
Can't talk now 'cuz I'm
Doing things no one else can do
Won't get done if I stop for you
Dishes piled up in the sink
Kids need bathed 'cuz they do stink
Laundry lays round like a worthless man
Do ya think he'd ever give a helpin' hand?
Tire is flat on the car
Know I'll not get very far
Play doll faces staring blankly at me
Toys are talkin'; how can that be?
Crazy is this life I know
Mommy is always on the go
Doctors, school, and grocery store
I'm worn and ask, What I'm livin' for?
Bills aren't getting paid
To brief my head was laid
To rest just for a li'l bit
But right back up I have to get
Privacy; tell me what is that?
Can't hide for a quick chat
Knockin' on the bathroom door
Little voices repeat once more
Begging again and again
Demands of me just won't end

—Your daughter

Call me when you have the time
I love you so much and I'm
Wondering just how are you

And say I really miss you too

Got the housecleaning done
Thought we'd go out and have some fun
Drive to the park or Cedar Lake
Hope you'll come and take a break

Sorry you're not feeling well
I'm tired too, can't you tell
Each priceless minute you speak
Are grains of sand I keep
That turn into a pearl for me
And string a mother tree

By your voice
By your time
By your hugs
By your smile
By your love; stronger be

—Your mother

Depend on Him

I don't like to be asking
But end up over tasking
When help I need; I do not ask for
Even though it becomes a greater chore
Doing it alone, and I overdo it
I should have waited, and I knew it

Making plans my own way
Can waste a gifted day
But when I ask the Lord His plan
My day is changed and understand
He has chosen many blessings for me
And guides me on a different journey

We can depend on Him; He wants us to
Knowing what is better for us than we do

He has overcome the world
Our Miracle Maker
When we are heavy-laden
Our Burden Taker

Through dependence on Him
Faith is made stronger
Endurance is gained
To function much longer

All things He can do for you
Depend on Him to get you through
Seek His will; watch what He'll do

When you can't move
He's the Earthshaker
When you can't see
He's the Open Eye Maker
Depend on Him alone
Our Safe Caretaker
When things get in our way
He's our Barrier Breaker

Depend on Him; He wants us to
Many blessings will come to you

Diamond Trees

Jeweled are the winter trees
In diamond chandeliers
No more emerald leaves
Until spring sheds her tears
She'll bring back her powers
Breathing life into the ground
Beating drums awake her flowers
I love that thundering sound
April feeds small buds in showers
And spreads her love around
But now the rain is freezing
They seem to be downhearted
The wintered trees; nonseizing
With burdened limbs have started
To break apart their necklaces
And fall to the earth's floor
Old Man Winter trespasses
To take their jewels once more
The trees look tired and mad
As if they have been crying
With broken limbs they're sad
But again will be glorifying
With sprouts of emerald green
Painted on leaves; all around
While April calms them serene
Breathing life back in the ground

Does She Know?

Too many sleepless nights deprive her of needed rest
Storms invade her mind; lightning strikes within her chest
Will joy come back and greet her and truly want to stay?
Or will the thunder of her soul wither her away?
Pain is her companion, but he is not her choice
She prefers to dance and sing but has a strained voice
Seems to her she does not matter to anyone
Hope hides beyond the clouds; oh, where is the sun?
Gloom is her blanket; bad dreams haunt her sleep
Alone in the darkness, I hear her spirit weep
I have wept with her, and I have touched her hand
Does she know I am with her? Does she understand?
I've cradled her in My arms and whispered, "I love you so."
I protect her from her enemies; she does not even know
Angels surround her, following wherever she may go
Her purpose is worthy of her; she's a chosen one
Gifted by "the Good Shepherd" before her life had begun
I watch her suffer through her doubt and all the fears
Her heart is torn by those she loves, kept in soul-drenched tears
Lost are so many loves, gone; yet held in her heart still
Just because they have died, they live in her and always will
They visit her often; sometimes she is unaware
Her life gets too busy to be still and knows they are there
Does she know there's a constant shadow of love
That brings a blessing when she is in need of?
Her needs are met, and she is protected
But she feels unwanted and so rejected
Does she know great things are coming her way?
Does she know I love her, and I'm with her to stay?
Does she know?
I love her, and I will watch her let it go

Draw Nearer

Draw near to Thee
My dear with Me
Sit and talk awhile
Hold My hand and smile
Know I hear and see
Trust alone in Me

I will supply your need each day
Read the Word and always pray
It strengthens you and helps you stay
Close to Me and brings you peace
Fix your thoughts; choose to release
Doubt or fear
I am here
Holy Spirit will guide
Prompting truth inside

Beloved, you are covered
I send My angels hovered
Over you and those you love
Always in the protection of
Those you release in My care
But you need to leave them there

Eternal Bliss

I have felt the deepest agony of losing my son
How did God feel sending His beloved one?

That sacrifice bore my every sin
So I can be joined with my son again

Eternal life was granted to me
He died for my life at Calvary

His love poured out in His shed blood
I am covered; purchased by the flood

Favored and forgiven, in His name
Forgotten by Him; there is no blame

Only He knows the pain in my heart
Missing my son is the hardest part

I know his perfect face I will see
A glorious homecoming that will be

This permanent void will be joy filled
To hold him again as God has willed

By His great gift of eternal bliss
For the Savior promised this
By my acceptance prayer
My home awaits me there

The Forgotten First Love

Spend time with those who inspire
Safe in the Circle of Fire
Protected by God's hand
Around you; angels band
Untouched by those so toxic
Who live a life chaotic
Lost and alone in misery
Their choices made draws them to be
Colored in shades of gray
Rebuke it; keep away

No matter what or who they are
Ignore their words spread like tar
Evil black as an empty hole
Lacking a joyful "living soul"

The saddest distance you may feel
When a loved one, but until
They find their way to Father Gold
Repent and in each heart enfold
"Spirit of life"; a new remold
Bring conviction of self-old
Making a change from bad behavior
Finding joy through "the Father's favor"

Returning to "the Forgotten First Love"
Father showers you from heaven above
More abundant than you're deserving of

Treasured Friends

Knowing your faults, they love you anyway
Your earth angels who hold your heart to pray
Their eyes see in you what others do not
Sometimes you feel they are all that you've got
They take your words into their own heart
Listening, without tearing you apart

Others are quick to judge what you will do
Thinking they stand so much higher than you
No time for them to love one another
By their blanket of judgment, they smother
Why pay the price for other's sin
Plotting against you time and again
Keep your distance from them; they'll not win

Stay close to those who are a rare treasure
Who *know* and *love* you beyond all measure
The ones who have eyes to see; ears to hear
Your loyal true friends who stay year after year
Who walk beside you and you both share "the light"
Like-minded in sisterhood; through "Spirit might"
Holy is this angel; God has sent to you
Sacred is the time we have and what we do
Praising Him for blessings, undeserving of
Like you, my sister, whom I so dearly love

Garden of God

Like seeds, we are planted on temporary ground
Sometimes uprooted to serve Him elsewhere
Transplanted by the breath of the Gardener
Winds preordained will carry us there

A flower does bloom in rich soil
That's watered most carefully
Planted for growth and design
Set into the place meant to be

You are the bud, the flower
By the hand of God, you're placed
Where you will grow and blossom
And your doubting is erased

Faith is the water to nourish
Your stem, your soul to rise
In success and favored
Held in The Gardener's eyes

The Garden of God is well-manicured
Although rock or weed may cause our fall
They can be our stepping stones, a stair
To see and reach our destiny call

His multicolored flowers
Cover the human race
Given all great powers
Whatever we may face

Storms will come and go
Or the weltered humid sun
He is our great ending
From where we had begun

A small seed, a tender bud
Planted right where you are
Never left untended
In bouquets, we go far

Joined with others in faith
We pray each other through
Thanking Him for blessings
In pruning how we grew
Obedient in His will
His protections over you

Standing high in The Garden of God
Stem to stem, hand to hand
Sister to sister, brother to brother
Heart to heart, I understand

Transplanting makes us grow and learn
To make new friends and gain insight
How we have come so far and grown
Nourished by His showering light

Gentleness

The way Jesus looks at you and me
And every child He's held on His knee

It's expressed on the face of a father
Who holds his crying newborn son
Shining from Mother Mary
When she nursed The Holy One

Angels glow; in softness, it is there
The way they move, how they care

In sweet tones of grandma's voice
Loving words by tended choice
Hushed over grandchild; her lullaby
To soothe them if they should cry

Gentleness
Heart caress

Raindrops lightly kiss your face
Tenderness found in a warm embrace
Cradled babe in arms of mother
A smile freely given to another

A nurse who takes hold of one's hands
Calming the quiver, patient understands
Pastor who prays with bowed head
Quieting a soul by words he said

In peaceful waters that reflect the moon
A ballet dance that ends too soon

Stillness of mild December night
Feathering snowfalls, ever light

Gentleness
How you bless

Father of the bride walking down the aisle
Daughters' hand held with heart-smile

Flickering candlelight
In the late of night
Casting shadows on bedroom wall
Lovers entwined relax and fall
Into a restful sleep
Same dreams they long to keep

How parents hold a child's photograph
Remembering how he made them laugh
Fondness of a memory
The youthful soul set free

Trickle of a brook under a covered bridge
In mellow flow over a limestone ridge

Shy little girl who peeks at you
Blowing not one kiss but two

Whispers carried on a summer breeze
Good manners asking, if you please
Gentleman's courtesy puts you at ease

Gentleness
Treated like a princess

Artist brushes her delicate strokes
Easy handed, water-colored pokes

Poets write with a gifted hand
Lyrics penned by God command

Graceful dancers waltzing slow
Move like waters changing flow
Steady in movement, both controlled
Pleasing to watch them enfold

Gardeners care in planting seeds
Nurturing soil, removing weeds
Bushes pruned, lawn manicured
Patience taken, hours endured

Gentleness
Ladylike noblest

Queen of England when placing her crown
That wave of hand, gracious in her gown
Noble acts done in secret
Touch you, and you don't forget

Loving care for an abandoned child
Rescued, held so tender mild
A helping hand to one quite small
Gentleness can do it all

Gift of Voice

Have you ever heard a song that made you cry?
Or a hymn that made you shiver?
Because the sound was angelic
And it caused your soul to quiver

Did the words so dearly bless your heart?
Or their message makes you fall apart?

That is the power in the gift of voice
With messages that prompt a memory
Either pleasing or unpleasant be

Assurance can always be found
In a hope-filled melody
Comforting to keep us sound
Of mind and spirit
Lifting us to a higher place
As you sit and hear it
Blessed by loving grace

If you have the gift of voice
Don't be afraid to share your gift
Sing from your heart, your spirit
God gave it so others could hear it

Gifts

The greatest of gifts is love
It is the reason Christ laid down His life
For all to be set free
Of sin at Calvary

It carried the cross
And nailed Him there
There is no other love so true
He's so in love with me and you

Every woman is given this gift
When she becomes a new mother
God lends them to us for a time
Each with purpose, like any other
All with talents God given
Created by Him to enjoy and love
A piece of Him, in the image of

Our gifts are to be used
Sometimes in greed
They are so abused
Gain not for His glory
We must give them back to Him
It changes your life's story
Rewarding is the gift that's given
To a needing heart and hand
Share what God has given you
He'll guide your path; design His plan

Some have the gift of service
God uses them in servanthood
With confidence in us

To give all that we should
It takes your dedication
It may take time from your days
But comes back to you in joyous ways

There are so many gifts
Yours are precious and rare
Utilize them freely
Bestow them with tender care
Unselfish in your offering
Expecting nothing in return
Giving is a blessing
A virtue we must learn
That builds character in you
By the noble acts we do

What are your gifts?
You may have many
Don't fool yourself
That you haven't any

Every person walking this earth
Was given gifts at their birth

It is in you to do great things
His gifts were not meant to keep
Their purpose is in the giving
You will sow what you reap

Glory of Heaven

Boundless in never-ending space
(Countless loved ones; alive in grace)
Sky-lit in breathing hues; ever glistening
Soaring in the air; all are listening
Song of saints and angels gleaming
Choir of voices beyond human dreaming
Only heard by the glory of heaven way
Carried on a shimmering light display
Celebrating life returned, to stay

Home again to the prepared place
You see His radiant face
Mansions of luscious decor
More than ever imagined before
With gifts awaiting those yet to return
Who still cry and have yet to learn

The glory of heaven
No more grieving be
The story of heaven
With a child on His knee
Worship Him holy

Painful memory cannot be kept
The Father dries all tears you've wept
Never sadness nor any fear
Left are earthly bodies; here
Changed; supernaturally
Heavenly bodies flying free
Soaring in never-ending space
Those we love so; *alive* in grace

Sweet glory of heaven
Home of the saved through Jesus Christ
By His life that He sacrificed
Great story of heaven
Oh, glory of heaven
That saved a sinner like me
Oh, glory! Glory! I'm set free

Glory to God

Gifted with the words to say
Guiding what I'll write today
I'm led in my poetry
It comes from God, not of me
Inspiring a story
To God be all the glory

He will send my spirit to travel
Collected diamonds spread like gravel
Are "precious truths," which brightly shine
I see and know His thoughts with mine
Each has its own purpose of healing
To mend a heartache I was feeling
I can see loved ones who have passed
Eyes of my spirit are steadfast
Fixed on all the beauty I have found
Floating above holy heaven ground
I am suspended in the air
I have no control when I'm There
My Father leads me
Glory to God be

Gardens There are so alive
Vibrant colors always thrive
Magnified in perfected hue
You'll see colors you never knew
They appear to have personality
With a voice to praise, miraculously
Flowers in a graceful ballet
Bow to Him as if to pray

Oh, praise Him when you awake
With the first deep breath you take
Sweet glory be; I've been set free
He breathes His life into me

Granted wisdom; for He is true
Answered prayers are followed through

God's Hand

In the wondrous glory of His command
He parted the sea with His open hand

Touching blinded eyes, He gave sight
His hand directs us to the light

It is tenderly placed on all newborns' hearts
As He whispers words of love in their ears
They *know* Him and the crying starts
That's why they cry their very first tears
His law of love is spoken to each one
It is then we are given our chosen gifts
And our purpose has already begun
God's hand directs, heals, provides, and lifts
All through the days and lives of every child
His instruction is to be meek and mild
We'll always belong to Him and no other
But must honor our father and mother

His eye is on us; He is everywhere
God's hand is outstretched, always reaching
When we lift our own hands in prayer
We learn through faith, His wise teaching

By open heart and hand, He sends "the Spirit"
To prompt us in good word and deed
Your heart knows to fulfill the act when you hear it
Reaching out to all those in need
His palm will grant a blessing on your head
If you chose never to turn it away
And you will stop to take the time instead
It returns multiplied another day

When we are found in sorrow, doubt, or fear
You will find God's hand for comfort near

He brings hope through our sorrows
In restorative tomorrows
In doubt, He builds our trust
Only fear the Lord; we must
Fear *no* man lest you be snared
Dear child of God, do not be scared

In the fear of the Lord, there is confidence strong
Where His children find refuge, to Him we belong

He will quiet you with His true love and peace
Correct that worry upon your release
The burden we need, not to bear
Let go and place it in His care
Sometimes we just won't leave it there

In God's hand
Understand
It's never empty or cold
Is anxious to unfold
And take a stronghold
Of your hand and walk you through
He is so in love with you

Goodbye to Summer

It is hard for me to say goodbye to summer
To watch the expiration of her last warm breath

Our separation purloins my joy and comfort
I mourn her passing on as a death

Leaves begin shedding from their trees
Like the disunion of children from their mother

The trees commence to naked limbs
Empty arms reaching out to one another

Is the winter snow an expurgation
To cleanse the earth
That unburdens the old and dying
To bestow new life
A virginal birth

Is that what our seasons are all about?
I've never seen it that way before
The serviced land retires with age
God presents His yearly offering
Fresh once more

Haiti Child

Home, it is all crumbled around me
Another earthquake
It took my mother and father
What else will it take?

I scream; I hear others wailing
I am so afraid
Nobody seems to hear our cries
For days I have laid
Under this debris
I'm so thirsty; my stomach twists
Please, someone find me

I may be a very young boy
But my spirit is strong
We are not rich people
Together we belong

Giving up is not in our blood
Courageous I will be
Until I am found, I'll lie here
And hope, my praying hands they'll see

I sing a new song of life
Making up each word
Trying with all my strength
My song must be heard

Voices are calling; I scream
Someone just touched my hand
Wake me from this bad dream
Help me to understand

My people don't give up
I know they never will
So many people cry
I'm speechless; I am still

Dead bodies lay in piles
All around me is death
A woman looks at me and smiles
Before she takes her last breath

Mother and father, I will do my best
To grow up fast; be a man
I'll dig your graves so you'll find rest
And except the Master's plan

He Lives

You gave me eyes that now can see
Ears to hear Your love songs to me
In my heart, I had prayed You there
Spirit moved me to show Your care
When kneeling down on the floor
I felt as if I could soar
Now I'm Yours forevermore

I am covered by Your blood
In the holy cleansing flood
Forgiven of sins You bore
Upon that cross and no more
Do You remember the stain
Washed by the bleeding rain
I am Yours, I'll always be
Hope of heaven, sing to me

His Face

I may have seen His likeness when looking at you
With holy radiance by the breath of Him too
Heart filled with the Spirit; righteous in your way
Guided by the Maker in the lifting words you say
I may have seen the twinkle from Bright Morning Star
Shining in the eyes of you; Christlike you are

He looks sun-kissed, healthy in style
Full lips colored wine in a majestic smile
His hair is long and wavy
And He looks tall to me

I love to hear His voice whisper through the pine
Softly reminding me, "Dear child, you are mine"
And in a tree the sparrow, He cares for there
His eye is upon him flying in the air

He cares for the sparrow; we mean so much more
Compassion shines about Him, all His saints adore
I've seen His eyes so kind; warm and deep
They hold you like a babe in mother's keep
A tender command of sweet invitation
There's no other love with His dedication
Held in His sight, a most precious treasure
I know that He's breathtaking beyond measure
With strong arms to cradle your every care away
And a voice that will melt you and beg you to stay

One day I will see the light of Him in His glory
And wonder no more how His eyes tell a story
Without the music of His voice
In the tale of His eyes, I'll rejoice

Looking upon His face
I'll be cradled in grace
Halleluiah
Halleluiah

His Plan Unfolding

You have been wronged
It is so unfair
But don't give up
God's hand is there

Do not be fearful
It takes joy away
For God is much greater
Than your worry each day

Remember, my dear friend
Your pain is promotion
To transform a better end
And change wrong emotion

Pray for a spirit of contentment
He will award you
If you rid yourself of resentment
God will see you through

If you're standing for Him
With meekness and control
Going out on a limb
To obey Spirit's role
It brings a calmer ending
And helps others to know
By your witness you're sending
His peace to overflow

Forgiving may be hard to do
But it will take your strength away
Releasing the power of you

To another every day
Don't give your power to someone
Who fights without a care
Pray for their peace, for they have none
Love them then and there

Do your best to be gentle and kind
To the person chained to their sin
Leave harsh words unspoken in your mind
May the Spirit guide you from within
And plant a seed of inspiration
To help that lost soul find their way
Left in their heart, the words you did say
That will bloom by the Spirit one day

His Precious Blood

Christ
By His precious blood that flowed from His veins
He covered and washed clean unholy stains

Redeemed by the shedding, without spot
As a lamb without blemish
Confessed sin is remembered, not

We are birthed anew and reborn from above
By remission of sin; forgiveness He bestows
Through His merciful justice and eternal love
Christians stand in the blood that flows
Free from blame in Jesus's name
In past, present, and future days
It shields us always in favored ways

You and I were purchased for God, by the Lamb
The New Covenant was forged in His blood
In His death and life for me; reborn I am
Saved by His precious blood; an ever-present flood
As powerful as the day He did die for *all* sin
That satisfied God's wrath; new life to begin
For His Son paid the penalty of death
Justification freed us by His last breath

"It is finished," were the last words He said
That first Good Friday He dropped His crowned head

Come to the cross to be cleansed of all your stains
That fountain that flows from the Saviors veins
You'll find peace with God, peace of Holy Spirit
That silences the devil's word; you'll not hear it

"Oh, Lamb of God, I come to thee
As I am, without one plea
Over evil I have victory
From sin, I am set free
Your precious blood was shed for me"

At the cross, we find *all* our needs
Past and presently it still bleeds
Found is a new living way
Covered by His blood each day

His Birth

Our Savior came to earth
Blessing Mary by His birth
This Lamb of God so small
Who grew so wise and tall
Became His mother's own salvation
The Great King of every nation
He came to earth as a man
It was the Father's own plan
That *all* sin He would bear
Love kept Him hanging there
No nail could ever hold His Son
My Bread of Life (His Holy One)
God's only Son Who set us free
Because He died for you and me
He was haloed with thorns as a crown
With blood tears on His face falling down
He said, "Forgive them for they know not what they do"
You could not bear the depth of His mighty love for you
A heart would truly break to *know* this passion of Christ
There's nothing we could do to change His love sacrificed
Because of His high thoughts and His heart of amazing grace
We receive undeserved blessings as we truly seek His face
Our Savior did come to earth
In the form of man at birth
To save all us sinners from a forever burning hell
Accept Him; confess your sin; be a servant who does well
Only God is *good*, for we can *never* say we are
But only set an example of Bright Morning Star

His Breath

I breathe in His breath so close to His face
Fellowshipping at the table of grace

With the Lion of the Tribe of Judah, I walk
Listening to His song; I love to hear Him talk

Circled by angels shouting their praise
Each face radiates a youthful gaze
Like a young one, my arms do raise
In a joyful dance; crowned in golden rays

No depth of love will you ever know
Or calming peace through you will flow
Then when you touch His face and see
The image of you and image of me
Christlike and somewhat the same
But only One King Who calls you by name

We wait for you; a celebration we plan
You will know the truth and understand

While in joyful dance; crowned in golden rays
Warmed by His love in your eternity days
Kissed by the Prince and angels aglow
His magic abides in an everlasting flow

His Love

His birth
Born to bring us salvation
King of every nation

His eyes
Are watching me
Protectively

His arms
Wrap me in tender care
Calming; to know He's there

His voice
Softly spoken; always gentle
Holy Spirit; within the vessel

His hands
Touch you and heal
Move at His will
Power you feel

His blood
On the cross was shed
Thorns crowned on His head
It was then that He bled
Still flows for you; red

His Word
Truth revealed
Prophetically sealed
Wisdom attained
Strength regained

Reading His Word
Out loud is heard
A song to sing and share
By His Words written there
In the Bible clear and strong
To guide us our lifelong

In His Loving Light

The wise men went to Bethlehem
There were three gifts they brought with them
Frankincense, gold, and fragrant myrrh
Jesus was in the arms of her
Mother Mary did proudly carry
The Perfect Son of God there
Who clutched a small lock of her hair
With newborn's eyes that shone so bright
He then *held* her in His loving light
Baby, Prince of Peace, has calmed this Christmas night

Kings and shepherds knelt in awestruck wonder
Profound as a heartbeat, drumming like thunder
All elated visitors bowed when they came
Kneeling before Him to praise His Holy Name

Angel Gabriel, who had come before to Mary
Told her to name Him Jesus, for this child she would carry
He will be a great man, Son of the Most High
She was a young virgin and did not know why
Or how she was chosen, then began to cry

Those months behind her, yet with her they would stay
And treasured up in her heart; the shepherd's words that day
With a message from an angel of the Lord, who stood before them
Bringing the good news of great joy; found for all, now in Bethlehem

And there He was, the baby Jesus
Sent to the earth; the One to free us

He will put far from us as the east is from the west
Our sins to be forgiven; He'll bear upon His chest

The heart of Him will break
When all our sins He'll take
Three nails won't keep Him on that cross of wood
Where His blood will flow, for only He could
Fulfill the promise of *love* that *kept* Him hanging there
The darkness and the thunder will be present everywhere

Mother Mary did proudly carry
The Perfect Son of God there
Who clutched a small lock of her hair
With newborn's eyes that shone so bright
He then *held* her in His loving light
Baby, Prince of Peace, has calmed this Christmas night
Profound is His heartbeat; Mary's song of gentle thunder
Her hair clutched in *the hand* of the world's wonder

Home to Stay

Remember me; I'm not gone
And I am not far away
God promised me long ago
I would be back home to stay
I belong to my loving Father
So I am where I truly belong
No longer am I sick or weak
Now I'm perfect, and I am strong
Remember I'm so close
I'll be near when you call my name
I laugh with my mom and dad
They look younger yet still the same
They've never looked more beautiful
I love looking at each face
I'm so alive, full of joy
And at home in this perfect place
God brought me home to stay
I dance with Brandon and Sam
We celebrate our lives
Rejoice with the Great I Am
My spirit sings; words unspoken
And you would be so surprised
What you do not understand now
One day will be realized
You'll have no doubt or sorrow
You will never shed a tear
Rejoice with me my loves
I am so happy here
One day, you will truly know
I live not very far away
When *life* takes you by the hand
And brings you all back home to stay

Hope in Heaven

Sweet uplifting hope of glory
Promises of heaven's story
Guide me through my everyday
To strengthen me along the way
Protected by the hand of God
Kept in His safe arms as I trod
On my life's journey to the end
To meet again, "Most Highest Friend"
And run into *His* arms of love
Where only truths are spoken of
No more lies, and no more sadness
No more evil; no more madness
Anchored hope in heaven; I am kept
Erased are tears of pain I have wept
I seek to find the light of His face
'Til I am found in His peaceful grace
Transported to a thanksgiving place
Undeserved blessings I'm grateful for
Flood my mind; spilling out my heart's door
When my purpose is needed no more
I will go to my great house of glory
Promised to me through biblical story
My hope is in heaven, all day long
He holds my hand and heart; His grip is strong

Hope

Have you ever found assurance in a song?
Had your heart awaited love and it came along?
Did you count upon a day
Then things went your way?

That is what hope brings
A human aid that sings
Is reparable of things
It solemnly swears
Corrects your affairs
Anticipates promotions
And eases your emotions

Hope assures; it grants; it lures
Is medic-able and it cures
Blessed assurance secures what hope is of
Hope is a golden seeker who finds awaited love

It is looking to find
With confidence in mind
And found is your pledge; a vow
In a rose-colored promise now
By word of honor; hope holds it true
Never give it up; it will hold you too

You're nourished in soul; through bereavement
Profited in useful achievement
Rewarded for a positive view
Blessed with favor over you
God sent by your hearts token
Kept hope filled; never broken
Your covenant bravely spoken

In heart word style dictation
Such hope can change a nation

It moves your soul toward its mending
Through joined hands saves the rending
Restoration ceases division's woe
Hope takes you where you need to go
Led forward with an angel made strides
Keeping you on joyous rides

Doubt will make you dreary
Discouraged and weary
Hold hope in sound conviction
Praise the benediction
Give thanks to God that your pledge, your vow
Brought rose-colored promises to you now
By word of honor; hope holds it true
Never give it up; it pulls us through

I'll Leave My Heart

I'll leave my heart with you here
So you'll not forget my love
It will hold you close my dear
Until we meet up above

Do not cry with sorrow
Rejoice for me in song
Some bright tomorrow
You will come along

I will wait for you
All of us will be
Together held so true
As a new family

What joy I do hold
As I run and sing
And never grow old
Fly without a wing
So brave and bold

No pain will grieve
Or tears I'll shed
My heart I leave
And these words said:

"I am where I want to be
I am home with family
I dance on pathways of gold
And laugh with mom and dad
All are youthful, not old
Be happy for us, not sad

It was always God's plan
He wants the best for me
I now can hold His hand
Joined with my family
I am home to stay
Be kind to others
This I do pray
Sisters and brothers
Please find your way
Back to me one day"

I Am Sorry, Lord

I make so many mistakes
I have caused others heartaches
To impatient when I need to wait
Missing opportunities and changed fate
My stubborn will gets in the way
Of plans You'll make for a special day
I leave Your gifts unopened there
And burden You with sorrowed care

You created me, for You love me so
Why You do, I just don't know
You enjoy my company
And always listen to me
Nobody loves or knows me as You do
You know everything thing about me too
But still, You love me *all* the time
Into Your arms, I want to climb
And have You hold me strong
Spirit guide to change my wrong

I know You laugh with me some days
It is then I feel *the Son-rays*
The warmth of You; held in grace
I long to be with You; touch Your face

Just hold me now and sing Your song
I wait to see You again; my wait's been long

Haiti Mother

Oh, God, my God of mercy
I hear her, but I can't see

My child, my sweet child
You are out of my reach
I can hear you crying for me
And dig so frantically

Mother is coming; hang on
Nothing can stop me now
I'll not give up on you
My heart is digging too

Don't be afraid my angel
My love will find you there
I will comfort you, dear
Keep calling so I can hear

Your voice is growing weaker
It won't be much longer
Somehow, I'm much stronger

Someone else is digging
Moving more debris
There's now an open space
I strain to touch your fingers
And then I see your face
Don't be afraid, my angel
My love has found you here
It can move a mountain
To get to you, baby dear

I bring you close to me
And thank my God of mercy
Wash your face with my tears
Kissing you ever gently
Away, away our fears

In Christ United

Born again as saved sinners
Chosen ones; we are winners
Having the greatest family
Any age or race; soulfully
All those who are a part of
One flesh, one blood, one love
Under one Godhead
Spirit-filled homestead
We fellowship in Christ united
Kindred souls; core ignited

And we fly
And we soar
And no more
Does one plod
But dance together
In the family of God

Before rebirth in spirit
We are spiritually dead
There's just one way to clear it
It's through Christ whose blood was shed
That is only the beginning
You pray Christ will forgive
And confess to Him your sinning
Asking Him to come and live
Live inside your heart
Thank Him that He died for you
Here comes the best part
You're saved from hell too
And you will live eternally
Always in God's family

And you'll fly
And you'll soar
And no more
Will you plod
But spirit dance
In the family of God

In Heaven

No evil words are spoken
No heart is ever broken
Never jealousy or hate
For loved ones; we wait

No sorrow; you'll not cry
No one asks, "Why?"
Truth and peace we breathe
Never wanting to leave
Not so far from where you are
Loves left behind, not out of mind
But alive in memory
In our hearts, they'll always be

Missing them, it's daily there
An empty room or chair
Baby cradle is still
Mother rocks it at will

Echoes of their laughter
Bring the tears after
Then I begin to pray
Lord, help me make it
Through another day

In One Accord

Fellowship has a sweet reward
Together in harmony
Gathered to worship for the Lord
Sovereign in His jubilee
Great joy we share in one accord

Hearts and hands are joined to pray
Edifying words we say
Are lifted to Him with song
The Lord makes the weak ones strong

Growing in the written Word
Shared testimonies are heard
Building others in faith and hope
Purpose filled to a greater scope
Knowing you are not alone there
When others open; choose to share
Trials they have made it through
Wiser while maturing too

Fellowship has a sweet reward
Praising together; one Lord
Braided with a golden cord
Love is bound in one accord

It Never Fails

Love never fails; it will change a life
Turn a woman into a wedded wife
Move a mountain to save your own child
Bringing peace to one that has gone wild

Love can tear down a big wall
Drives you to give it your all
Forgives a hurtful pain
And bow for others gain
Give someone else the glory
Keep quiet the real story

Holding hands through the storm
Joined hearts feel safe and warm
It calms the thunder of one's fear
Reassuring them, "I am here"

It composes the sweetest songs
And makes right all oppressive wrongs
It embraces the unlovable
Can answer the unsolvable
Free easy; the unlockable

Love never fails; it's like a ladder
Climb together; you're less sadder
Marching upward, catching a star
Brighter your thoughts, joyful you are
Thankful that you have come so far

In words; effectively inspires
In hearts; induce native wildfires
The truest love never retires

Is never jealous but admires
Makes you honest; pity the liars

When good friends wish, you make it theirs
Love is greater when made in pairs
Glued together and never tears
Helps the elderly up the stairs
Prompts the husband to do his repairs
Keeps him from awful cheating affairs
His love never fails; he always cares

It colors your world a golden hue
Love is planting a garden for two
Growing a rich harvest within you
Returns all the selfless deeds you do
Prays the undeserving through
Is open to a child's point of view

Gives freely an honest blessing
Comforts a loved one whose stressing
Kind words flow while you're expressing
How you care with hands caressing
Put an end to second-guessing

Build up someone's self-esteem
Guide them to fulfill a dream
Give it passion like lovemaking
Praise all the steps they are taking
Make good what their heart longs for
Found is victory and more
Blessed you are each year start reliving
Love never fails in dear heart giving

A mother's tears will carve a mighty river
Her love prayer causes the child to quiver
Protective words, the Master will deliver

Guarded under His wing; holding their hand
'Til He calls one home to the Promised Land

It never fails; Christ's never-ending love
Sustains a mother when she has to let go of
A beautiful child she loved so deep
But went to heaven in God's keep

John 8:12

Oh, how precious the light of life
The mind brought out of darkness

Renewed in thought and spirit
Shrouded by it; daily near it

So I sing to the Lord
Looking up and toward

The smile on His face
Lighting up with grace

Joy

I feel it when my children laugh
The sun shines from their face
It's in the song of a child
Of any language or race

Joy weaves through your opened heart
When you kiss your newborn's head
It is there with such excitement
With the first word he has said

I find it in the simple things
A shared smile or small gift
Thankful for great blessings
That give my heart a lift

It gently blows my hair
When I stand under the moon
With a breath from heaven
As summer leaves too soon

A garden full of flowers
That brings a hummingbird
Evokes my heart a waltzing
In flight of wings, I've heard
Fluttering so fast and free
Overcoming her shyness
Flying to the breath of me
Close to my nose and eyes
It fans my very face
So small and mighty
Quick in her race
To me then to the flower

I delight in her grace
And the sharing of her power

You'll find the greatest joy
Is found in selfless giving
From the heart of you
It's when you're truly living
Stop and help the stranded
Expect nothing in return
Give to the empty-handed
Help the lost to learn

Your reward is pure joy
We all need that each day
It is most precious
When we bless it away

It comes back sevenfold
When it comes from your heart
The sweetest stories ever told
Is of the joy one had shared
Who took the time to stop
And showed them you cared

Have you seen a rainbow
Through the cleansing rain
After a hard day's work
That left you in pain
But seeing that rainbow
Brought to you a thought
The joy of our Father
He forgets us not
Reminding us of joy
Wherever we may go
Delighting in His sight
The joy He wants us to know

Kindred Spirits

Connected in spirit before birth
We knew we would leave that Holy Place
And vowed we would meet again on earth
It was then that we first saw His face

Remembering His voice; we cried our first cry
Because back to arms, we wanted to fly
After He whispered sacred words so clear,
"You are My miracle; I have sent you here"
We then play in our mind a great memory
Of home in heaven and how it used to be

Now I have a vessel to house my spirit
I grew so fast in an unfamiliar space
With mother's "heart song," I could always hear it
Above my head in a warm cocoon place
That very gentle drumming that I loved so
Grew fainter when my water cradle let go
I learned fond scent in the arms of mother
Preferring it first then to any other
And returned was heart song back to me
Joined with "my mothered" harmony

Time has gone by, and my vessel has been changed
Bearing my own children gets things rearranged
We are like a flower that can bloom anywhere
Transplanted by Father; His hand is always there

This temporary journey led me back to you
I treasure all our time and the things we do
Talking and laughing or sharing the love of the Lord
As kindred spirits reunited in one accord

My friends, brothers, and sisters in Christ

Land of Life

Heaven is the only place
Where joy is constant on each face
When forever becomes a life
Eternal joy an end of strife

Saints and angels as true friends
With no occasion of demands
There is no "want or need"
All souls are truly freed

Abiding always is joy and love
Alive in resplendent praising of
One King, one Savior, one Shepherd
The Way, the Life, the Truth is heard

No evil word is ever spoken
A heart would never be broken
Mended is all that we use to know
Sorrow and pain are let go
Forgotten is any past evil or grief
You mustn't be sad; embrace relief

Your loved one is in the Land of Life
Living in joy; late husband or wife
Your child is in the sweet care of another
More precious to Him than you, his mother
Where Grandpa and Grandma wait for you there
The dance of life and joy is an endless affair

Dry your tears and honor each one by name
By their gifts, live through the same
As if they were here, and so they are

Alive in memory, as a shining star
Continue those gifts, give back their love
You will not regret the giving of

Their purpose continues through
The lives of loved ones they knew
By planting joy through your sorrow
That strengthens every tomorrow

Hope is found in giving not taking
Even though your heart may be breaking
You are never alone in your sadness
Even though you cry in madness
Begging for the pain to end for you
And that void will be filled too

Joy for your sorrow will be replaced
By healing tears shed open-faced
And the Father holds out His hand
For only He does understand
And He cares for you so much
Within reach is His touch

Living in the Present

Limited we are under time and space
Dependent on the present with God
The now gift today must stay in its place
Not yet in the future do we trod

God walks with us in the now
That is where He is today
You can change the future; how?
Wait for Him to guide your way

The present is a gift
Live one day at a time and free
Your future; just uplift
Give it to God, and you will see

Peace will come; do not worry
Tomorrow's not been met
Be calm and not in a hurry
To run ahead and fret
Anxious as you scurry
Future is not here yet

God is in the here and now
That is where He'll be
Pray for strength; He'll show you how
To set future free

Love

Love is the One who set me free
When He came and died for me
It is Father, Son, and Holy Ghost
Never is arrogant nor does it boast
Powerful in what it is and does
It's the greatest gift that is or was
It's building up, not tearing down
Giving a smile, changing a frown
Thinks not of one's self but of others
Is the purpose of many mothers
Thoughtful and never smothers
Showing kindness to one who won't
Works to finish what others don't
Sends prayers for those who choose to hate
Is patient so others don't have to wait
Shows up on time, doesn't want to be late
Endures all things
Sells wedding rings
Makes family time
Creates a passionate rhyme
Tickles your toes
Kisses your nose
Gives you a rose

Dries shed tears
Casts out fears
Calls you my dearest friend
Finds the best card to send
Or makes their very own
Saying this is a gift, not a loan
Waved in sweet baby kisses blown
Gives earned raises

Sings holy praises
Reaches out to the needy
Isn't selfish or greedy
Guards her child from any danger
Has compassion for a stranger
Meets man and wife, lip to lip
Leaves your waitress a good tip
Happily gives much of their time
Spends on you their very last dime
Is always faithful and true
Sees only the good in you
Grateful to serve and be your host
Fries your eggs and butters your toast
Kisses scrapes so they'll heal
Does not have the heart to steal

Sews you quilts and pretty clothes
Wipes your tears and dirty nose
Tucks you into bed at night
Paints gray skies so sunny bright

Praises and does not criticize
Delights in truth but never lies
Plays music that feeds the spirit
Turns from evil, won't get near it
Forgives beyond sevenfold
A grudge, it will never hold
Is glad to meet you where you are
Scrapes the ice off of your car

Makes up the difference at the store
When money's short, you got no more
Bakes cookies for an elderly neighbor
Believes her child was worth long labor
Thanks others for good deeds
Plants flowers and pulls weeds

Sews masterpieces without a machine
Changes diapers and keeps baby clean
It's spoken in words to help and heal
Never to hinder or crush one's will

Resists temptation to do wrong
Composes hope in a Christian song
Makes you dance, keeps you strong
It never fails and will not abuse
Nor takes advantage or ever use
Embodies miracles beyond belief
Shares the burden through your grief
Hugs the cold, unhuggable people
Raises hands to build a church steeple

Giving the best instead of money
A secret ingredient in making honey
When a heart listens with open ears
Why Father Daddy sheds mercy tears
It's Who takes us to eternity
And forgave our sins at Calvary

Brings sweet peace in a deep spirit yawn
Mows the neighbors before your own lawn
Procreates through fruitful spawn
Gave the blind their sight
Cradles you at night
Love may ask but never demand
Makes me stop at a lemonade stand
Tells those kids to keep the change
Lets your schedule rearrange

Works for others because they're sick
Wakes you up with a puppy dog lick
Gives a dead battery a jump start
Keeps children's laughter in your heart

Lets coworkers take a break
Cleans a mess you did not make
Whispers hope to show you care
Braids your little sister's hair
Writes tender words for a song
Romances lovers all night long

Devotion of man's fidelity
Honors vows dutifully
Keeps you up all night with child
When tears and temps go wild
Carries out wishes of the dying
Forgives someone who left you crying
Gives up a bad habit for you
Teaches toddlers to tie a shoe
Thinks what Jesus would do
Cares for animals at the zoo
Guides young minds in Sunday school
Obeys and lives the Golden Rule
It searches for the best day care
Missing them while they are there

Makes me hug my mom and dad
Touches your heart to see the sad

Falling head over heels for you
It's why two answer; yes, I do
What blessed the child in the womb
Why Jesus rose and left the tomb
To leave and prepare the mansions above
For saved souls raptured to live in love
Awarded the purpose of your life
Provided for the widowed wife
Why father works overtime
How you have the strength to climb

Quivers the body and the heart
Wraps two souls who cannot part
Takes their breath yet makes them stronger
Makes them live so much longer
Molds them into one frame
United by Mr. and Mrs. Name
Wraps bride and groom in passion
Love is always in fashion

The sweet spice in your mother's cooking
Presented to you so delectable looking
It rubs your back; right- or left-handed
Pulls you over to help the stranded

Keeps you safe and warm on Daddy's lap
Wrapped in a sweet dream as you both nap
Love is the greatest gift to be given away
Binding souls while hand joined to pray

Love is the greatest gift given
Christ dying for the sinful, liven
By His love, we are forgiven

Love Bouquets

Share your God-given powers
Plant bouquets of flowers
Lend others a helping hand
Extended for one to stand
Be a guiding light
Pray them through their fight
Whether loss or despair
Make the time; show you care
Listen with the very heart of you
Never judging what they say or do
Ask for God's protection; pray them through

Use your purpose for His glory
Rewrite pages of your story
Make changes in your behavior
It shrouds you in the Lord's favor
Difficult it may be
To let your own will free
By faith, we grow
We may not know
Or understand
What is His plan
But we must always hold hope
Anchored by His grace to cope

With every loss, there is gain
The sun reappears after the rain
In rain of tears that fall down
You shall be blessed with a crown
Renewing you; feeling much stronger
Now released; you carry no longer

Left at the foot of the cross to bear
That is why our Lord chose to hang there

Share your God-given powers
Plant bouquets of flowers
Water the seeds with love
And watch the blooming of
God's wonderful grace
Glowing on each face

Made Strong

When I am weak, He makes me strong
Depending on Him all day long
Be open to His power
To blossom like a flower
With a purpose to fulfill
Allowing the Lord's will
He'll prepare your day ahead
Provide your daily bread
Make your dreams come true
He connects with you
When you surrender with your heart
By way of Spirit; never part
Holy Spirit will guide you through
Ask the Lord what He'd have you do
Following His trusting lead
Blessing you with all you need

When you are weak, He'll make you strong
He will uphold you all day long
Trust in His mighty power
You are His precious flower
Grow and bloom right where you are
Your worth is more than a star
He named each one in the sky
He loves us so; you and I

Miss Jealousy

This wretched monster, ugly, green-eyed
Commits many crimes after she has spied
Miss Right who she wishes she could be
But knows she has not the personality
So her wicked mind begins the game
Trying hard to put Miss Right to shame
Spreading lies and making fun of her
Miss Jealousy always fails to conquer
Her devious pursuits are carried too far
She can't accept any shining star
Miss Right
She wants to be right where you are
Her animal behavior is so bizarre
Repugnant are her thoughts each day
She never has kind words to say
Deliberate ignorance is her way
Never sure of herself, always in doubt
Just angry vulgar words belched out
Miss Right makes you look so weak
She stands in truth, modest, and meek
You fall from lies and you stumble
With barnyard words, you grumble
You lack her tolerance and grace
And you'll never have her sweet face
Possessing beauty with a patient smile
Nothing you've done has been worthwhile

You're just more homely inside and out
Decay is what you are all about
Wish you could accept what you see
In the mirror and just be happy
Take better care of your sad looks

Eat better and read self-help books
Exercise and learn new makeup schemes
Try positive words and take up dreams
That moves you to heroic places
Change your screwed-up faces
Pray for help and just be true
To yourself and all others too
Give a great smile when others frown
Be courageous and turn around
Looking in the mirror you'll see
Miss Right and no more Miss Jealousy

More than a Memory

Mother did you know I have kissed your face while you slumbered?
I am close, yet I am not so far that I cannot still be yours to love
I am right here, Mom, and it is but a whisper

I carry your smile with me
How could I forget my mother's face? I never could

Fractions of time flash like a light
It is more than a memory; it is *love*
A constant living breathing awareness
Like a breath, a breeze, a gentle tide rushing in to enfold you
And glazed are the waters of love, like the reflection of the moon
It is carried in the current, the power, the flow; the connection

I remember what I should and what is
My brothers and sisters, I love with a greater depth and understanding
Can you tell them this?

Most Faithful Friend

Oh, Wonderful Counselor
Your living word directs my way
You teach me through the day
Prompt or warn me when I pray
Where I shall go or if I'll stay
If I should wait and just be still
And be obedient in Your will
My Everlasting Father
I am your child; You love me so
Father Daddy, I want You to know
You're the gentle brook of my spirit
Dayspring visits from on high
Unveil the truth, and I fly
Soul kissed in tender mercy
I hear *the amen* speak to me
Witness—faithful and true
My Good Shepard guides me through
Sweet bread of life
I shall not hunger or thirst for
Believing in Him, the Door
By Him, I entered in
The Savior of my sin

Good Shepherd of His sheep
He calleth by name
They know His voice
No other is the same
Only a stranger is heard
If known not the Word
Compassionate Servant
The beloved in healing and serving
The broken, the blind, or undeserving

This Man of Sorrows knows grief
He carries me to belief
Trusting in my Prince of Peace
My soul quiets with release
At His feet, I lay my sorrow
Sharing secrets of tomorrow
How I hurt and why I cry
I miss loved ones and ask why
How can people be so unkind?
Hatred masks their eyes blind
Powerless is their mind
To know the passion in love or death
In the giving or the taking away
What power is held in words we say
I may rejoice or grief today

I may be reminded by a song
My loved one has been gone too long
It doesn't change the missing them so
Wanting to but afraid to let go
I don't want to forget and fade them out
Others don't understand what I'm about
My mind so clear I see their faces
Remember shared words, favorite places
But can't recall the last minute or two
Rescue me, Lord, I sorely need You
They judge my leaving in thought
Ridicule me and forgive me not
I try to be meek as a lamb
Give me strength, Great I Am
To love them with Your heart and spirit
Heal my mind; I need to clear it
I want to live with love surrounded
I'm locked in the closet of "lost and unfounded"
Fight these battles, for I am too weak
Give me healing precious words to speak

Holy Spirit, feed my empty core
I'm dying to be found and lost no more

Chief Cornerstone
Tear down my walls
Lift me up from my falls
Build me a foundation; One Spirit filled
By the Father, framed and goodwilled
Teacher
A teacher come from God above
I'm your pupil; school me in love
Train me in the wisdom of Your word
Grant my memory what I've heard
To be absorbed and keep its place
Hold me tender in Your grace
Save my children; they'll see Your face
Enlighten them with the truth
Keep their souls in youth
But their minds; wisdom of light
To my grandchildren, give story
Through vision, blessing, and glory
Reveal my love when I don't know how
Open my soul's eyes and theirs now
I don't know when You'll call my name
I cannot leave them feeling blame
For what I may have said or done
I love them so; bless everyone

My Redeemer
You paid my ransom, love set me free
Unchained my soul, paid a price for me
I am forgiven, and I'm unbound
Nails held my sin, my scars unfound
You bear the scarring marks of love
So I could live eternal with You above

Mother's Love

There is no end or limit
No action or word could dim it
Its depth lives beyond her heart
Past any distant star
Mother's love is a silent prayer
That covers you where you are
A constant sacred whispering
Sometimes you may not hear
Because of other voices
Tugging at your ear
My love is much greater
Than any form of hate
That's why it's hard to wait
Before I can hear your voice
Or plant a kiss on your face
I hold you always in my heart
Kept in a most honored place
This is how much I love you
You can't believe its power
God hears my spirit whisper
Every sleeping and waking hour
Mother's prayers of love
Touch the heart of God
It is the sweet thought of
Mother Mary's love

Granddaughter

The softest curls crown her head
Cascade and frame her angelic face

Her eyes invite my heart to hold her
In my arms, she finds her safe place

So warm and shielded in my care
She bows her head into the heart of me
Her gentle words sound like a prayer
On my lap, she dreams happily

I drift back as I watch her sleeping
To my arms when holding another
While she was in my safekeeping
Smiling at the image of her mother

Only a mother knows this kind of love
And I wonder what she is dreaming of

My Wife's Voice

I call her name; where is my wife?
She doesn't respond to me
Twisted metal and concrete
Have crushed my left knee

The earth is shaking again
Dirt fills my nose and eyes
It's hard to breathe it in
But harder to hear those cries

Hours and days they've screamed
My wife's voice, I do not hear
I pray for her, not myself
Because of what I fear

I fear I may have lost her
But I can't give up now
My family needs me
I'll make it out somehow

This is my second nightmare
It happened here before
I'll not leave my homeland
I would be home no more

This is where I was born
My people are so strong
And this is where I will die
Because here is where I belong

I think about my wife
And in my mind so clear

I see the light of her smile
And her calming voice I hear

Walking through the concrete
Twisted metal and steel
I surrender to her calling
No more pain do I feel

My Journey's End

When my life's journey comes to an end
Leaving my family and every friend
What will they remember? What will they do?
Will they say, "My Lord sustained me"
With all that I went through
Trusting in Him only and seeking His face
Longing to be held in His arms of grace

Will they know I loved them always?
No matter our good or bad days
What they did or what they said
If I caused the tears they shed

They may forget the poems I've written
And forget my name
But I pray they remember
My Most Loyal Friend
When my life's journey comes to an end

That they will seek You every day
Guarding the words they chose to say
Trusting in You and the written Word
Praying and sharing what they have heard
When Holy Spirit speaks out loud
Be confident to share in a crowd

My life is in Your hands, Lord
And daily I'm looking forward
When I can touch Your face
Walk beside You with grace
Returning heaven-bound
Were I'm home
Safe and sound

A New Beginning

Be grateful for each day, each hour that you are breathing
Thankful for blessings, by God's grace we are receiving
Wait for His voice and reach for His hand
Call out His name, so you'll understand
That you are not alone in your battles or sorrow
He will fight for you and plan a better tomorrow
If you give up your own to follow His will
Learn to be patient; sometimes we must be still
Endurance we will find when we hold hope
Through the struggle you held tight the rope
Like an anchor of our soul, steadfast and sure
He calms us with His loving presence—so pure
Love one another, honor father and mother
Obey the thoughts He will create in your mind
These are sacred words to teach us to be kind
To learn to forgive when your heart is broken
Replacing those chains with a golden token
That surround your soul in a holy light
Wings carry the burden with great might
Soaring like an eagle away from our sight
Time will heal the wounds if we just let them go
Never to return and stronger we will grow
Finding ourselves in a more peaceful place
Releasing the weight of every chain link
When we obey what the Spirit does think

Spend focused time with Father every day
Be gentle and careful in the words you say
They possess a power when given away
To bless others if we speak them with our love
Instead of harsh words, we should never speak of
I have so much to learn, and I'm growing too

Be patient, Lord, and hold me closer to You
When I begin to fall, which I often do
So I will stop and take the time to be filled
With the *knowing* of my purpose; You have willed
Teach me to love the person, cut by their sin
And focus on the person "I am" within
To give up my will and change my behavior
Growing closer to You, my Loving Savior
Keep my children safe in your loving care
Family and friends keep closely planted there
Help me to let go of what I have held too tight
What never was mine; I need to get this right
And become the woman You have intended
Loved ones gone; You temporarily lent
Never belonging to me; this I knew
Light the rest of my journey, in all I do
Until my life ends and I return to You

No Tomorrow

If I do not see tomorrow
I'll leave behind all sorrow
An enter into my eternity
My joy in heaven waits for me

I will see His shining face
Surrounded by loving grace
Held in His arms; such sweet embrace

Reunited with angels and my loved ones there
I'll remember those I left in His protective care

We may not know what tomorrow has in store
Or the purpose of our lives we are living for
But we all have gifts to use and share
Through prayers and faith, we will get there
To the end of our journey and return
To Our Creator and then we'll learn
How He placed us in so many ways
On paths we crossed that strengthened our days

One God

Halleluiah! Halleluiah! Halleluiah!
Angels sing in adoration
To God of man; God of every nation
All saints praise in celebration

He's so much brighter than any star
God is always right where you are
My Heavenly Father
Your reach is never far
Far from me
You'll never be

Halleluiah! Halleluiah! Halleluiah!
Creator of the universe
Maker of night and day
Great eagles in high flying
Know You and know their way
Soaring higher into Your cloud
Sheltered in nest; defended proud

Fish swim long in the sea
All aware of His majesty
In open fields, the cattle graze
A newborn calf wobbles as he plays
Like an infant's precious first step days
And learn when they keep on trying
Sprout new wings and end up flying
God grants His power
Likewise, a budding flower
Tender blooms branch out like hands
Waving at Father, who understands

Halleluiah! Halleluiah! Halleluiah!
Angels sing in adoration
To God of man; God of every nation
All saints praise in celebration

Halleluiah! Halleluiah! Halleluiah!
Halleluiah! Halleluiah! Halleluiah!

Only in My Dreams

I knew you were out in the world somewhere
A soul mate who also prayed for me there
Into your strong arms to hold and rescue me
Never imagining how perfect we'd be

I could sense you close when I closed my eyes
You were so much more than I visualized

My heart held the hope that you would find your way
I'll not forget the first time; that blessed day
When we saw each other, and that moment we knew
Your prayers said for me joined my prayers for you

Neither felt worthy of such a mighty love
You were so much greater than I had dreamed of
My life changed from darkness to constant sunshine
How could I be your s and how could you be mine

You took away my very breath when you'd just smile at me
And tell me all the time that you were never so happy

Often we would speak out loud the very same thoughts
Laughing and sharing a bouquet of forget-me-nots
Memories that crowned our heads and bound us so tight
Stronger, through your prayers knelt beside me at night

Reading from our Bible while snuggled in bed
I listened to the promises written in red
Spirit filled with love by the words Jesus had said

Your voice was like an angel so tranquil to my spirit
I loved the scent of you, always needing to be near it

We lit hours on fire until we were both spent
Talking and laughing, then asking where had the time went

Only in my dreams could I have thought this to come true
When our hearts held the sweetest hope
You loving me
Me loving you

In loving memory of my late husband
Edwin Lawrence Toney
Murdered August of 1980

Others Could Not Hear

His home is made of cardboard brown
Snow has frozen it to the ground
He dreams of his mother now with her Lord
The One she prayed to, looked up toward

When she would tuck him in at night
Her smile warmed him by the candlelight
Great stories he would listen to
His mother's love he always knew
Her last words were, "I love you"

No other person understands
His grunts, waving of hands
No word has he ever spoken
And now his heart is broken
She was his voice; he had heard
He could not reply in word

Mothers heart had a gifted ear
To hear what others could not hear
His dancing hands she understood
Answering, as only she could

She cared for him for thirty years
And gently washed his dirty tears
That fell from a puzzled face
Mean people are such a disgrace
Gathered ignorance in a crowd
Pointing at him, laughing out loud
Throwing mud and bruising stones
To see his tears shed through moans

No school had he ever attended
Nor boy or girl he had befriended
On mother he fully depended

Awakened from his wintered dream
Because he thought he heard a scream
And realized he made that sound
For no one else was to be found

He tried again to scream "that Name"
The One mother called, then He came
He took her three months ago
The One she prayed to, soft and low

With all his might he let out a long scream
And seemed to have fallen into a dream
He spoke "that Name," loud and clear
That's how mother brought Him near
His eyes were closed or he thought so
He saw a man that he should know

He was there at his mother's side
The One called Lord, and then he cried
No tears he shed but words spilled out
This is "The Lord" she talked about

He felt so calm in warm surprise
As if mother had washed his eyes
Again to see more clearly there
The Lord appeared up in the air

With such brilliant light around His frame
He heard Him softly call out his name
Appearing before him an angel came
He felt a peace he never knew before
And wasn't cold or afraid anymore

She took his hand, and they began to soar
So quickly they arrived at a great hill
Then he saw her; he could not be still
Into the arms of his mother, he ran so fast
Together, *home sweet home* at last

Peace

Peace is felt the deepest in the presence of God
It's what cradles your baby with a sleeping smile
And keeps a pastor knowing his work is worthwhile
Befriends lovers while moonlight walking
Surrounds me when angels are talking
It weaves into the mother from her newborn's breath
Glowing softly in the dance of a candle's flame
Envelops heart and spirit in Jesus's name
Peace feathers all of the angels' wings
Lulls the babe when Grandma sings
In that warm friendly feeling of being home
Loving awareness I am never alone
The play of rain in a soft piano tone
That radiant look on a spirit-filled face
Serene breezes, taking you to another place
Knowing your children are home safe
Blessed thoughts that start your day
Found in your soul when you pray

It will be what you feel when you see Jesus
Fresh sweet calm after a storm
Restful nesting in being warm
Heavenly view of waltzing meadows
Cascading waterfalls and gentle brooks
In a gentle way, an angel looks
A sacred companion on a country drive
It's in soothing melodies
Peace rocks me in safekeeping
Holds me close while I'm sleeping
Wraps you in cashmere thought
Velvet hugged in forget me not
Peace is heart and mind kissing

Knowing God is always listening
And He is with me where I go
Peace *is* the prince you need to know
It's the song of the birds when on my walks
The message of love when my Lord talks
Reminding me I'm in His care
Peace is knowing He's always there

Power of Spirit

My eyes see quite differently
Than someone standing next to me
Spirit moves me like a prayer
At any time or anywhere
Holy Spirit whispers a lot
Sharing a message, waves of thought
Into the ears of my own soul
Now knowing God is in control
To purpose-fill, transform the day
Direct His plan and light my way
Moving me in one direction
Leading me by His reflection
His thoughts are higher than my mind
And when I leave my own behind
Revealed are treasures I will find
When I yield to His loving grace
He leads me to a "healing place"
To meet a new earth angel's face

Like the mother who lost her son
For I lost two, not one
We talked for hours; time went fast
"When do you stop grieving?" she asked

Losing a child carves a deep wound
Through mother's tears, we are cocooned
Held by Our Father in His care
No greater burden could I bear

With hope anchored I was sustained
In every loss, something's gained
Strength renewed by us letting go

He was never mine; this I know

Through visions, God gifted to me
My son tells me he's so happy
He visits anytime or place
How comforting to see his face
His joy *sun-shines* in my heart
To heal the time we are apart

On spirit travels, I've been sent
Not always knowing what they meant
Having no control over where I went
Yet humbled by the time I spent

Transported once to a war-torn land
I witnessed buildings crushed to sand
Nothing stood where it used to stand
I found a boy so scared and small
Hiding against the tallest wall
Not more than three feet was left there
Dust covered his skin and black hair
His big dark eyes glossed in a stare
With arms crossing his knees to chest
My soul felt what he's expressed
And lifted a prayer request

In transit to a living room
My spirit sensed a heavy gloom
A little girl with long blond hair
Sat on a piano bench there
Her grandma sat down, down by her side
And held her gently as she cried
For her mom and dad had both died
Grandma was the mother of one
Her daughter was her setting sun
Years had passed I found after

Teenaged face now full of laughter
After praying and wondering how
The both of them were doing now
Her eyes so blue and skin so fair
I'd recognize her anywhere

These visions are so perfectly clear
I could not see or could not hear
With my human eyes, earth's vessel
By His power, they are nestled
I can't forget; my soul has seen
My core holds them in deepest green
It is my color of healing
Which prompts a reborn feeling
Bringing renewal and rebirth
Like the spring that changes His earth
In calming hue, He paints the trees
And meadows raised up to my knees
It is life, everlasting true
Budding hope, petals blossom you

One night when I closed my eyes to pray
An instant vision began to display
I saw Jesus walking my way
At the bottom of a great hill
I was in awe, and I stood still
There was a big lion, settled by a tree
To my left, and sitting to the right of me
Was the whitest lamb you ever will see
My feet were on a well-worn path
I felt warm in a glowing bath
But then it vanished way too fast
Oh, how I wanted that calm to last

The second time there was a change
It touched me too, but it was strange

Jesus walked nearer, so carefree
Lion and lamb stood smiling happily

My last vision was number three
(The sign of Holy Trinity)
I watched Jesus, lion, and lamb
While focused on the Great I Am
In the great distance, I could see
A large crowd to welcome me
While in this vision proposed
My prayer eyes were still closed
I tried very hard to make out their faces
They were too far away for familiar traces
With eyes and frames of those I love so
But I couldn't see who I would know

The power of Spirit is a being
The third person I'm seeing
Father, Son, and Holy Ghost
His voice, my Heavenly Host
Prompts me with His command
Leading me to understand
Obeying what I hear spoken in my soul
Gives Spirit the power to take control

He has changed who I used to be
And touched the very core of me
I see things with "Spirit's eyes"
The gift of truth; no lies
I am lifted with each surprise

The power of spirit
His voice, stay near it
Open to, never fear it

You grow in faith, hope, and peace

This Counselor helps release
Your own will or desires
Allowing you to walk through fires
Untouched and protected
When Holy Spirit was not rejected

Praise His Name

When you arise, seek His face
Let His light fill your space
Surrounded by His grace
Tranquil in the knowing
His plans for my growing
Are by faith that brings to me
Answered prayers by my plea
Ask and you shall receive
In waiting you believe
He will bless you even more
Then what you had prayed for
With patience, we will find our way
Wait on the Lord; He's chosen the day
To bring to your goodness by His glory
Praise His name and share the good story
Of Jesus's love that nailed Him to a tree
That is why He so willingly
Came as a man to set you free
Free from sin and gifts to use
In your purpose, you mustn't refuse
To give those gifts back in return
To God give the glory, then you learn
Through sharing, others are blessed
It comes from God; He'll do the rest
You've done your part, though it be small
God used you, and through it all
You must not stand with pride
But be humbled inside
Praise Him everyday
In daily words you say
Praise His holy name
You won't stay the same

Praise You, Lord

Praise You for this day
This day that You have made
Grateful for the way
You calm me in the shade

Turned my life to merriment
Replaced money I have spent
On someone else, I could not afford
Heart giving has such a sweet reward
Praise You; I thank You, Lord

I am broke, no food to eat
My neighbor comes with a treat
Homemade soup and banana bread
I won't be hungry when I go to bed

Praise You, Lord, for angels on earth
I value their treasures worth
More than I could return
From the little that I earn
But You show me ways to bless
And help me to make progress

On prayers, that's how my car runs
Can't fix it; don't have the funds
I have a job I'm thankful for
And legs to walk out the door
Into the light of Your sun
With eyes to see a child in fun
Skipping on a summer day
And I can hear what angels say

So glad I can write and read
That You supply what I need
To turn the radio on in time
For a song that helps me climb
To a higher place
Blessed by Your grace
A message sent for hope
It lifts me, helps me cope
With what I'm going through
I'm grateful, Lord; I praise You

Quiet Time

Begin your day in the most calming way
Read a devotion book and take a look
In the Written Word; His voice is heard

Commands and instructions light up your mind
Be undisturbed, leaving other tasks behind
Absorb His joy, what treasures you'll find

He will brighten up the most deary day
The light of His presence on you will stay
His peace strengthens you while on your way
To find the blessings He's planned for you
Another day of growing in what you do
Chose to be thankful and help others too

Quiet time should not be mistaking
Selfish or lazy in moments you're making
We all need a time to be still
Devoted to Him, in His will

Let no one or nothing take it away
Make quiet time a gift today
You give to Him and to you
Time with Him gets us through

He opens doors you should not close
Opportunities for you; He knows
Will help you prosper in the end
He wants to be your best friend
Helping you attain your goals
Choosing to save lost souls

The path may be hard to trod
Don't give up, you have God
The creator of all things good
Obey the Holy Spirit
Do well when you hear it
There is a reason for each command
His help is there, holding your hand

Pray for the lost
Give at all cost
Make a change
To rearrange
Goodness to cover evil
Calm the upheaval
Quieted in your way
With gentle words you say

The Bible is living water for the soul
Bread of life will feed you; give Him all control

Reborn

I found You just in time
After a long hill climb
Drowning in my wine
Taking what wasn't mine

Too many drugs messed up my head
In the hospital, I was pronounced dead
I traveled far through a tunnel charred black
I heard wretched screams and begged to go back

Falling down in that hideous nightmare
Creatures were biting and pulling my hair
Kicked and beaten while I was down there
I cried out to the Jesus of my mother
She always prayed to Him and no other

"Jesus of my mother, please save me today!"
A strobe of light beamed down and took me away
I stood at the end of my hospital bed
Mother was crying; a deep prayer she said
Holding my hand then kissed twice my forehead

I felt right away a burning in my chest
Though weakened and startled; I had been refreshed
It's hard for me to explain
I was elated in my pain

Opening my eyes, I saw my mother's face
Feeling for the first time, her spirit of grace
I cried quilt tears of shame that brought a great relief
Knowing I had caused my mom enormous grief
But she never turned her back on me

A mother's heart can always see
Within the heart of her child
Though confused and wild

Praying me up the long hill climb
Found I was and just in time

I took my mother's hand, and we prayed
Holy Spirit came; in my heart, He stayed
Reborn I am; a sinner saved
Finding hope my soul had craved
Lost no more, for I have been found
Cleansed by His blood that still pours down

I had a hunger, thirsting for knowledge
(Not in the fundamentals of college)
Reading the Holy Bible is the way I survived
Quenching a dry soul; my spirit was revived

Infallible wisdom, truth, and history
God's law, will, and correct morality
Love, faith, hope, patience, joy, and direction
I was learning the calm in deep reflection
Never in greater peace have I been sustained
From drugs and alcohol, I've refrained
Staying clean with joy in the Lord
My strength renewed and looking toward
My future days without fear
I'm born again; I see clear
Before I was so blinded
Always selfish, close-minded
I am free; now I am free
My Lord lifted and carried me
Out of the darkness into His light
The eyes of my soul are opened bright

Rescue Me

I am drowning in this sorrow
Lord, bring me hope for tomorrow
Release this arrow from my heart
My love is gone; I'm torn apart
I am proud he served our country brave
Now part of me is buried in his grave
He fought a cause called freedom
My Lord, I really need some
Free me of battles in my head
As I hold the last words he said

I'm so empty and cannot sleep
It seems all I can do is weep
I can't concentrate anymore
Just sitting here, I watch the door
As if I'm dreaming and will awake
And he'll walk in to gently take
My hand and we'll join in prayer
I wait and wait, but he's not there

My thoughts are all a cloudy haze
The hours keep adding to my days
Rescue me; I've got a war-torn heart
Show me, Lord, where do I start
To pick up the pieces left of me
Able to breathe again and be
Much stronger for my family

Bless all others who feel alone
When loved ones did not come home

Roseman

I am a long bridge in Winterset
In case you and I have not met
I'll tell you stories you'll not forget
I've watched so many people come and go
Those who come from town; some I don't know
I see all kinds of the human race
And I remember with joy each face
They walk through; I have no door
I don't mind footprints on my floor
They sometimes leave their autograph
Tickling my walls to make me laugh
I watch the little children as they play
Removing shoes on a hot summer day
Wading through my gentle brook
Underneath me, they will look
For rounded stones, they can throw
To skip across the waters flow
I have so many loyal friends
Joy is mine; it never ends
A couple shares their wedding day
Father of the bride gives her away
Mother doe comes with her fawn
They nap together on my lawn
Nestled in the green lap of me
Sheltered by my wooden belly
I am here through every season
Visit me for any reason
I am Roseman; tall and wide
I stand with Winterset pride
I welcome you to come inside

Run to Me

You have run so very far
You don't know who
Or what you are

Lost in the fast pace
Hurried every day
To finish a rat race
And don't take time to pray

You worry so about your debt
Recklessly, your money is spent
And wonder why your goals aren't met
Don't stop to think about the rent

Anxiety plays with your mind
Your thoughts like a glass shattered
Forgetting things that truly mattered

The car has a flat tire
There's no food for dinner
You walk on a tight wire
And you're growing thinner
The stress makes your body ache
So tired but cannot sleep
How much more can you take
You ask yourself and weep

Then you receive His answer clear
I'm waiting for you to run to me
I will hold you, child; so dear
And ease your misery

I'll fight your battles, see you through
Provide your food and give rest
Honor My will, not the will of you
For your life is truly blessed

What you need you have now
I want to remind you
When I see your head bow
To be thankful too

You have run so very far
You don't know who
Or what you are

My child, you are My own
Leave your burden in My care
Know you are never alone
My love covers you there

Run to Me; My arms are open wide
Talk to Me; I listen while you confide

Sacred Day

She lies on an old quilt upon her brother's grave
Although she weeps, I tell myself she is brave
I can see and faintly hear my daughter singing
And sense from a distance the angels she is bringing
It is the Sabbath; a beautiful day
I rejoice, not because you've gone away
But in such sacred thought I stay
Knowing you're where you want to be
And that very thought just lifted me!
You shine, adorned in a jeweled crown
I'm drawn to the circle God sent down
Soul invitation takes me to your sister's side
She looks oh-so-lovely even though she has cried
I listen to a song and close my eyes
Joined in reverence, my spirit flies
Dancing in a ring the angels fly above
My smile is wide and warmed in love
You're next to me, your sister too
Joyance lights up all over you
I want to keep my eyes closed tight
And take in all the showered light
I feel the breath of heaven overflow
Raptured in the life you know
Only a glimpse of how you're living
Brought my heart such peace-giving
A healing that touched me this sacred day
Did shroud me tender as we drove away

Seek His Face

His presence is with me
Here, continually
Beaming with His glory
My joy is from the Lord
Seeking Him; look up toward
His face to shine on you
Stay in the Word and do
What we're commanded to
You may fall short, but preserver
Stay strong in Him, He loves us dear
Knowing we may stumble
Be patient and humble
Others will condemn your belief
Stand firm in joy; no grief
Disapprovals, there will be
In Christianity
Suffering; while many die
Belief in one God; that's why
No statue or piece of wood
Would save us; nor ever could
Seek His face; the image of
The only God; God of love

For Christ's sake, we delight in weakness
Insulted, yet you'll stay in meekness
This does not make you weak but stronger
Jesus has suffered so much longer
The world hated Him first; some still do
Seek His face, and let it shine through you
Speak His name, and He'll be there
Keep your enemy in prayer
Leave them behind you in His fire

Their cause is evil with desire
To hurt you because they are lost
Soul-dead and they shall pay the cost
It is through empty words they have said
Which reveals the unsaved; spirit-dead
Seek His face every day
Guard the words to choose to say
And for your enemy; pray
Ask Holy Spirit to stay

Sister

I may know you as part of my family
Having the same mother
Or someone else you might be

Sisterhood is found
On solid ground
Whether blood shared
Between the two
Or not the same as you

It is in the connection
Not seeing your reflection
As in the sister of your childhood
With the same DNA, if you would
But through a purposed meeting
A new sister you are greeting
It is not by chance
You take a second glance
God planned it to be
A new sister you'd be

Destined to be a long-time friend
Or chosen for a season that will end

A sister is your sweetest pal
Possibly a crazy gal
But she always has your back
Gives to you what you lack
Helps you shine like a star
Sisters, grateful you are

Her eyes are brown and skin is too
She looks so different from you
You both were born the month of June
Twins in soul so much in tune

I was born the month of May
My eyes are a deep blue-gray
I am white, but she does not care
A sister will always be there

You may live so far away
Always in my heart, you stay
Though you may have lost touch
You love each other so much

Losing a sister who is now with the Lord
You keep her in memory and look toward
The day when you will meet again
And hold the hand of sister-friend

The sisters you grew up with and knew
May not be most sacred to you
Not one could take their place
You miss their presence; each face

Life can change your sisterhood
Love them as you should
Even though you seem far apart
Keep them close in your heart

This world is changing, just be strong
Pray for each sister all year long
Leave them in His loving care
When they chose not to be there
Love them anyway
Whether they stray
Or come back to you one day

Sit with Me

I love it when you are still
Resting in My presence true
While seeking out My will
Allowing Me to guide you
Sit with Me in My loving arm's chair
Faith kept only in Me is best
Depend on Me for your every care
Give them to Me so you'll find rest
Empty hours and days; you have spent
Sleepless with heartaches, you worry
My angels guard you; bound in My tent
But you're always in a hurry
I patiently wait for you to ask
"Lord, show me what You would have me do"
Stop and think about each meaningless task
Are there more worthy things I've planned for you
Sit with Me, and I'll sing you My song
Spirit will direct your path today
I will stay with you the whole day long
'Til darkness of worry fades away
Keep your trust in Me; keep Me nearer
Our sacred moments help Me prepare
Your day ahead, which holds Me dearer
More intimate when invited there
My child, I'll follow you anywhere

Song of a Warrior

I am a warrior
Youthful and strong
Standing firm on the rock
To Him, I belong
The belt of truth is fastened
With breastplate in place
No worry of sinking sand
Held in His saving grace

I run and not grow weary
Like an eagle, I can soar
I am blessed abundantly
By His love forevermore
His Word and thought renew me

Given a sound mind
Power of spirit and love
Past is left behind
Future is not thought of

When living in the present
This very day He has made
Life is much more pleasant
When you need not be afraid

I am the righteousness of God in Christ
Jesus knew no sin yet paid the penalty
He died for all and by His sacrifice
I died with Him my savior; my sin set free

He rose again on my behalf, for He loves me so
My salvation is from Him, my Lord

He lives in my heart, and He will never let me go
In His presence, I'm led forward

Nothing I've accomplished am I deserving of
His works which were completed for me
By the shedding of His blood and eternal love
Old things passed away; no longer be
Reconciled to God through Christ
His precious gift of eternity
The promise of paradise

I am a warrior, youthful and strong
Soaring like an eagle to where I belong
Back home to You, and You'll sing Your love song

Song of Joanne

With sharpness of mind, I am spiritually aware
Awakened in perfection beyond all compare
Such grandness my eyes do behold
All are youthful; not one is old
Each living and breathing in this massive place
Endless joy is mine—kept in a loving embrace
I ran to Him, and He touched my face!

You will love the living gardens; I walk through
Breath of the flowers reminded scent of you
Colored stars do shine, yet no night here
Twinkling as your eyes and brings you near

I've learned much in little time and know
Love takes us when we're meant to go
My life lived out with purpose; then done
And return again to where I had begun
Home in the arms of "Great Holy One"

Celebrations abound; peaceful truth found
Circling, soaring round and round
Flying near the laughter of you
Most precious song I ever knew
Loved ones wait; as I am waiting too
I'll take your hand, Joanne, and fly with you

In the song of Joanne; the angels celebrate
Your laughter reaches heaven, and here I wait

Song of Joy

Praises ring, oh, how they ring
Can you hear the angels sing?
Born is our Savior—the King

And in the sky a star so bright
That signaled His birth that night

Perfect Son of God
We sing for You with joy
Mary cradles Him
This precious baby boy

She lays Him in His manger bed
Joseph gently kisses His head

Shepherds were tending their sheep
In the fields near Bethlehem
An angel appeared to them
To share the good news of Him
They could find Jesus in a manger of hay
Glory to God in the highest
A group of angels came to say
And on earth peace, goodwill toward men

Wise men came to worship Him
Gifts of gold and myrrh they brought there
Burning frankincense to sweeten the air

Praises ring, oh, how they ring
Born to us, Almighty King
Perfect Son of God
We sing for You with joy

Mary cradles Him
This precious baby boy

His scent of heaven, in holiness there
She breathes with Him, so much to bear
How could she be the chosen one
For God the Father sent His Son
By the Holy Spirit conceived
And how was she to be believed
That God sent Him to earth
Born of virginal birth
Her body was the powered vessel
The womb of her for Christ to nestle
Now He cries outside the womb
At the inn, there was no room

A feeding trough, His manger bed
This Prince of Peace came humbly led

Born to us a Savior, to set us free
The Promised Anointed One is He
The King above any other kings
So let the praises ring, ring, ring
In songs of joy, we sing, sing, sing

Perfect Son of God
We sing for You; our joy
Mary cradles Him
Oh, precious baby boy

Songs of Beauty

My newborn embraced close, sweetest breath of a dream
A brook flowing gently over pebbles downstream
Whippoorwill soothing me when he will call
Melody of leaves in chase as they fall
Pitter pat of rain, dancing on the ground
Laughter of small children playing around
So happy and carefree
Blowing kisses aired to me
Shatter of squirrels racing each other
Lullabies like a prayer from grandmother
Cooing of mourning doves at early dawn
Their unique "winged" sound landing on my lawn
Tickle of soft breezes waved through my hair
Flutter of the hummingbird in the air
Running down the track, whistling of a train
Symphony of a storm with thundering rain
Coyotes howling in the night
Underneath a moon that's full and bright
Voice of an angel, lit in a golden hue
Or gathered together in a room with you
Horses neighing that run so free
Cherished old hymns when sung to me
Your child's bowed head to pray out loud
Your heart plays a song titled "Proud"

A field of wildflowers in sunshine dance
Wave like hands joined in summer romance
Deer panting to drink at farmer's pond
Wide doe-eyed, so innocently fond
Lying by the fireplace, warm and tranquil
It flickers and crackles until
Ashes go to sleep after you do

Held by the one so in love with you
Bible reading, "Sword of the Spirit"
The Word of God, to speak or hear it
Poetry and songs of praise to read
Songs of beauty, something we all need
Church bells ringing; a bride and groom are wed
Sacred are the vows that in truth are said
Drumbeat of mother's heart, while inside her womb
Pavarotti singing in my living room
The ocean rushing to the shore in praise
Waving higher as in voice to raise
It's song to God because it knows
He created their body that flows
Trees do sing and mountains quake
Joined in choir for heaven's sake
To God in purpose to glorify
All He has created; that is why
Birds sing as they soar up to His sky

Newborns know; that's why they've cried
To hear His voice at their mother's side
Bending down to baby's ear
God whispers, "I have sent you here"
You are My miracle; My own
You still belong to me
I lend you to her now, my child
A gift you are to be
One day you will return, My love
Where life began with Me above

The voice of God is everywhere
Breathing His beauty through the air
The wind, the rain, the skies so great
In songs of beauty when you wait
Take time and listen, look and see
The wonderful songs of beauty

Spirit Flight

Let my spirit fly
I pray again to soar
I promise not to cry
Can't hurt like this anymore
Take me to my healing place
Where You've taken me before
To look upon each joyous face

My two sons, my mom and dad
To the sweetest love that I ever knew
Thoughts of him color me sad
Then remind myself; he's happy with You
His death left me a lost widowed wife
You sustained me, oh, Lord, and held me through
There in every loss of my life

Let my spirit fly
Father, let me soar
Where I've been before
Beyond heaven's door

To Grandpa Plennie there
Whose faith was great and ever strong
He'd sit beside me, and we'd share
Piano benched while singing song
("What a friend we have in Jesus
All our sins and griefs to bear")
It's been years, but I tear up still
For I knew that he loved me so
I miss Plennie; I always will
The Plennie Blunt some use to know

As a pastor in a church that still stands
I remember his safe praying hands

I'd run to him and Uncle Dean
Dad's brother, Uncle Shorty too
I'd laugh with all in fields of green
Grandma Frances, I will dance with you

I'll walk gardens with Nancy Marie
An earth angel God had sent to me
Boarding at the Chicago O'Hare
And flew to Washington, D.C.
For a poet's symposium there

Sam and Brandon, I can't wait to hold
Still young and looking much the same
In bodies healed that don't grow old
Shining as I call them by name

Mom and Dad, so youthful in glory
Are living their eternal reward
Joined in sister, brotherhood story
As one family of the Lord

I'll see again, the sweet love I knew
And his voice will call out to me
All his wounds were healed by You
Transformed in mind with a new body

Let my spirit fly
Past the clouds
Beyond the sky
I will not cry
Let my spirit fly to my healing place
Where perfect love shines from every face

Travels of My Soul

Sweet uplifting of my soul
Makes me soar, fills me whole

Rushing like a river strong
My spirit becomes a song
It takes me where I belong

Reaching heights beyond the sky
My soul has eyes when I fly

I go to unknown places
And see unfamiliar faces

My journey may be far
Or close to where you are

Revealed are joys unending
Spirit words are mending

What I lost, can be found
Truth is told, bold and sound
Reassuring all the way
Calming me, I want to stay

Out of my body, left behind
So vivid and clear is my mind
It just happens; I've no control
The many travels of my soul

Sweet Baby Lord of Love

We sing to you a lullaby
You shine for all though You may cry
Sweet baby Lord of love
Sweet baby Lord of love
As a lamp illuminates the darkest of places
You will light up this world by Your mercy and grace us

Changing history
Born to misery
Our Savior we have met
Oh, how could one forget
How He paid our sin debt

Word became flesh; among us He dwelt
What abandonment His Son deeply felt
The disciples asleep, while on His knees He knelt
His soul so very sorrowful, even to death be
Praying to the Father, "Let this cup pass from me"
Then returned to pray there, in Gethsemane
Still sleeping was Peter and two sons of Zebedee

His most agonizing pain; none other has ever known
And by His sacrifice, the greatest gift of love was shown
God's victory over death of sin, cleansed me as His own
Water from his broken heart wept, with the blood that had flown
Yielding to His suffocation, to save us by His death
Eternal life was gifted me when He drew His last breath

Bright Morning Star
Is what You are
Our Light of Dawn
In our hearts drawn

Kindling a royal flame
Powerful is Your name
Jesus! Jesus! No other is the same

Sweet baby Lord of love
Sweet baby Lord of love
The Purest One; Little Lamb
Born to us; the Great I Am

Almighty King; not one shall reign above
When perfect love was born; spirit-birthed-of
Sinless in His way, from that very day
Sent by God's glory
Our Christmas story
As a lamp illuminates the darkest of places
He lights up the world by His mercy to grace us

Take It, Lord

This day is yours; You already have it planned
Help me walk with You; against evil take my stand
May the Spirit hold my tongue; no harsh words said
Take all negative thoughts; replace them in my head
With the words of great wisdom that you speak
Take burdens from me, for I am too weak

Remind me when I get too busy that you still care
My work will be more pleasant feeling You there
I then will feel the calm in the tasks that I do
If I stop and be open to the presence of You

Satan attacks with deceit and lies
He has his own evil-minded spies
They spill their words with ugly decay
To rob my mind of tranquility each day
Take it, Lord, so I'll not repeat what they say
I want no more battles; I'm trying to change
Aid my mind with soul to clear and rearrange
The thoughts that are not mine, but spoken
That may leave me confused or heartbroken

Many blessings and gifts I'm not worthy of
You gave them to be returned to You with love
Take it, Lord; my very selfish way
Hold my head down when I pray
Your hand on me will guide me in Your Word
Forgive my ignoring; the Spirit I've heard

When I disobey the knowing to complete a task
I just don't take the time to do what You ask
Take it, Lord; this wrong behavior

I want to be in Your favor
But I am too stubborn in my own will
To busy myself and not be still
I need Your strength with me until
I carry out what You needed right then
So I'll be renewed; seek Your face again

Take it, Lord; my selfish sinning way
Forgive me; make me stronger each day
I really need this change in my behavior
Tuck me in Your wing, my loving Savior

Temples of My Soul

Sacred rooms hold my mother and father
My children and grandchildren live there
You would not believe the colors
Or the hymns that always play
I love You that is where You'll stay
Sisters and brothers, friends new and old
All earth angels forever I hold
There's always room, yet no vacancy
Filled with sunshine, sweet fragrance be
Like holy water that keeps blessing me

Temples of my soul
Are what I have, what I am
Never empty, always whole

Pictures hang, memories live forever
Laughter paints a wall with sunny hue
There's no ceiling, floor, or corner
It's never-ending because of You

The Lord's Plan

Enjoy the road ahead of you
No matter the twists and turns
It all has a purpose in your life
Seek with your heart the Lord's plan
He'll guide so you'll understand

You were sent to earth with a purpose
Creating you to be loved
Given to you were gifts to use
They are to be shared, not kept
He whispers to you while you've slept

You are His greatest miracle
He told you this at your birth
And you do not remember
But that is when you cried out
We knew then what it was about

He created you so He could love you
Then He died for you on the cross
The price paid for all our sin
Pray for direction on life's path
Be slow in judgment and in wrath

Forgive those who always hurt you
And bless them with your own heart
We never know when we leave them
If it might be our very last
Let go of the hurt and the past

Serve God and others with much care
Be a servant not a beggar

Be thankful for all you have
What you need you already possess
And miracles never second guess

Enjoy the road ahead of you
Even when you don't understand
God has your purpose in His plan

The Serpent

A mask of deception he wears
On his journey of evil affairs
Causing such pain and fear
The wicked liar creeps near
To the innocent or those who follow him
Taking truth and joy to leave them grim
Faith is tested beyond belief
Weak in spirit have no relief
In darkness, all followers dwell
Their destiny is one of hell
Tortured in pain, constant fire
Caused by the most wicked liar

Those who go to the Rock and stand
Will find there, strength and God's command
Strong in spirit will not fall
Faith is strengthened like a wall
Built to shelter and protect His sheep
What God promises, He surely will keep

The serpent's path will lead you to death
Let no evil word poison your breath
No thought or deed causes you to stray
Follow the Good Shepherd every day

Believe in what you do not see
Faith brings all that's meant to be
Be strong in the Lord and be true
You'll find a more Christlike you

The Great I Am

His righteous right hand upholds me
His thoughts help me think more clearly
Through His eyes, I see differently

I am protected as His lamb
Held tender by the Great I Am
Good Shepherd who in His tending
Keeps His flock, love never-ending

The Good Shepherd who laid down His life
For His sheep
Know His voice and will follow Him
Held in His keep

Safe and sound
In Him; I found
Rescued from my enemy
He moves me toward safety
His Spirit guides, which lives in me

Through Him and by His command
I learn and lean; can understand
What He will do? What He has planned?

I am undeserving of His marvelous grace
Enjoined by His angels in charge, guarding my space
The day will come when I'll touch His beautiful face
Returned where I began; into His arms, I'll race

Until that day, teach me, my Lord, to be
More Christlike, a greater change in me
Dying to myself, surrendered in Your will
Ending my journey when my heart becomes still

The Reason Why

Most Precious Promise there ever was; will ever be
Is this Christ child I carried inside of me
I hold You lovingly; You search my face
And wish I could have birthed You another place
But You are here, and so am I
Joseph holds Your tiny hand
And then we cry
We cry, cry, cry
Our tears of joy
He is joy, joy, joy
Most Precious Promise
Sweet little baby boy

With a yawn, I thought I saw You smile
Stretching out Your arms to the sky
I just want to hold You, Jesus, for a while
Humbled to be chosen; don't know *the reason why*

You are not mine to keep
Softly for You, I weep
You are God's only Son
His Beloved One

Joseph whispers into Your ear
So softly that I could not hear
Laying You in Your manger bed
I quietly asked what he said

You grabbed his finger and didn't let go
And believed I did not need to know

Most Precious Promise there ever was; will ever be
Is this Christ child; kept in the heart of me

The Holy One
Emmanuel; "God is with us"
His only Son
Emmanuel; rejoice in thus

Hallelujah
Great psalms of joy
We bow to thee
Prince baby boy
On bended knee

All angels sing in praise of You
Shepherds and kings in chorus too
Surrounded in Your shining light
Born to us this Christmas night

With a yawn, He smiled so bright
And stretched His arms up to the sky
Most Precious Promise in God's sight
Christ knew the truth; *the reason why*
Born God-Man to die

True Friends

Knowing your faults; they love you anyway
Your earth angels who hold your heart to pray
Their eyes see in you what others do not
Sometimes you feel they are all you've got
They take your words into their soul and heart
Listening without tearing you apart
Others are quick to judge what you may do
Thinking they stand so much higher than you
No time for them to love one another
By their blanket of judgment, they smother
Why pay the price of someone else's sin
Plotting against you time and time again?
Keep your distance from those who just can't win
Stay close to those who are a rare treasure
Who know and love you beyond all measure
The ones who have eyes to see; ears to hear
Your treasured friends who stay year after year
Standing strong beside you at the same height
Stay in Spirit's power with all your might
Earth angels who hold your heart to pray
May be called home on any given day
Be true to those who love you just as you are
Even when they leave, they are never very far
Always in their prayers, day after day
Loving you through what you do or say

Unworthy of His Love

Always; I have been misunderstood
I knew I was different somehow
It started when I was so very small
My life's journey has been painful for me
But it has been truly extraordinary

My favored playmates were angels
They never judged me or made me cry
We loved one another and had such fun
I thought angels appeared to everyone

They always listened when I spoke
Numerous times I have been spared
With vital protection; loyal and strong
Angels guarded me all childhood long

Their voices are gentle and reassuring
Captivating in a *presence*, so alluring

I went to church and said my prayers
I felt God always listened to me then
But it wasn't until I was an adult
I accepted Jesus Christ as my Savior
My eyes and heart were open to favor
It caused me to change my behavior

I knelt beside Sister Laura Anderson
It was November seventh of 1972
After I prayed, I began to cry
I told her I felt like I could fly

She said, "That is the Holy Spirit in you"
It changed my heart and gave me conviction
To alter my thoughts and how I dressed too
As if I had been blind and now could see
I heard another voice that embodied me

The Holy Spirit *is* a person, a being
A someone and He is very real
It is the Creator; my God who is love
The Holy Trinity; the three persons of
The Father, the Son, and the Holy Spirit
God sent Him; His voice, I hear it

I'm a saved sinner, born again
Don't look to me for perfection
I will fail you; I fail my Lord
Yet still love-wrapped by a golden cord

Jesus died on the cross for our sins
He came as a man to die for me
I caused His flesh to be whipped and torn
I put that crown of thorns on His head
He carried my heavy cross as He bled

Those nail scars; one day I shall see
A reminder of His sacrifice for me
I will touch His head that bears a crown
Marked by the thorns beaten down
I will be a witness too
A pierced sword that went into
His side that poured out blood and water
Water from His broken heart; the slaughter
All His wounds; the scars He'll bear
His love alone kept Him nailed there
For no nail, no man, no power could ever be

Greater than the will of my Savior
Who died because He is so in love with you
And so in love with me!

Amen!

Vision of Three

One night when I closed my eyes to pray
An instant vision began to display
I saw Jesus walking my way
When I reached the top of a massive hill
I stood in humbled awe, and I was still
There was a big lion settled by a tree
To my left, and sitting to the right of me
Was the whitest lamb I ever did see
My feet were planted on a well-worn path
Washing over me in a peaceful bath
But then it vanished way too fast
How I wanted the calm to last

The second time there was a change
It touched me too but it seemed strange
The lion and lamb stood, smiling happily
With Jesus, they came so very close to me
By His side; like friends they walked
I believed they could have talked

My third vision was somewhat longer
Afterward, I felt so much stronger
Just to see His most handsome face
I'll not forget Him or that place

I watched Jesus; lion and lamb
While focused on the Great I Am
In the distance, I saw so dimly
A large crowd behind Him and He
Turned around to them then back at me

I tried so very hard to make out any faces
They were too far away for familiar traces
With eyes and frames of those I love so
But wasn't able to see who I would know

While in this vision proposed
My praying eyes were still closed
I opened them with wonder: questioning awhile
Why did the lion and lamb look at me and smile?
Was the well-worn path made by centuries dated
By those who have gone before me and have waited?

Can't forget the way Jesus looked at me when there
With His eyes so kind, long robe and wavy hair
Sandals He wore on His feet
Most faithful friend I'll ever meet

Voice of God

If in the darkness, now you trod
Beckon the light and voice of God
Surrender to Him and find your way
Accept Him into your life today
Ask forgiveness of sin to be set free
You're made stronger, and wiser you will be
Growing in the Words of truth
Transformed and returned to youth
Renewed in mind and soul
Give to God full control
Your thoughts will start changing for the better
Read scriptures daily like a love letter
The Spirit will guide you; you're godsent
You can depend on Him to the end
There is no greater teacher or friend
Yield to the teachings as lessons are learned
Abundant are the blessings we've not earned
But by His grace, we're saved and protected
Living close to Him, never rejected
Return to the One, your first love
Who loves you over and above
Your human comprehension could not understand
The voice of God will lead you; move you by His hand

Wealth

Being rich is not in money or material things
A castle, Lamborghini, or vintage diamond rings
It is held in the treasure of who and what you are
Spirit shining bright as an "all-day" star
Unselfish in giving; kindness pours from the heart of you
Your friends are like-minded, moral in what they say and do

Good deeds are done without expecting a reward
Paying a stranger's way; pray they pay it forward
The simple things in life mean so much more
Wealthy by taking in what others take granted for
Moment by moment through your everyday
Pocketing fortunes along life's highway
You stop to give the Father time and say,
"Thank you for Your gifts of abundance I see
Deposits made freely; *payrolled* to me"

The setting sun, flowers, and song of the bird
Flying close to heaven, for God's voice they've heard
Limbed trees of emerald green bow and know
By His hand are stronger as they grow
Lion and lamb nap together in His field
Farmed crops through labor, produced a good yield

Mother holds child; though doctor said she could not bear
Wealth is gifted to us by way of God-share
Giving and receiving we find treasures of joy
Richly awarded with a little girl or boy

Gifts are given abundantly; to you, to me
Those not blinded by greed who can clearly see
Wealth is measured in who and what you are

Spirit shining bright as an "all-day" star
Wealthy by taking in what others take granted for
By way of God-shared gifts; I could not ask for more

I already have more than what I need
Wealth is found in giving, not in selfish greed

When Jesus Died

The skies turned black while the earth did quake
Upon the last breath, He did take
That very moment brought victory
Death was destroyed and sin set free!

He emptied Himself of power, to bear
Your debt of sin that left Him hanging there
He looked down at His mother as she cried
The sword of her pain cut Him inside
Mary knew it was God's own plan
Jesus was born to be a man
And humbled Himself to the sum of death
Therefore, God exalted His name in breath

As higher than any other name spoken
In heaven, under, and on the earth
No other name compares in power or worth

When Love Listens

You tried to talk to a coworker today
About an incident and wanted her to pray
But she ignored you and just walked away

Your husband came home to you in tears
You began to share hidden fears
For you had held it in for years
He felt the problem he had to solve
Interrupting your words to resolve
With dissected words, he did involve
Her husband was not interested
Her pain was further nested
The only thing she wanted him to do
Was listen to what she was going through

Three doctors you tried so hard to tell
That you had not been feeling well
So discouraged your spirit fell
The fourth one you begged him, "PLEASE!"
Listen to my symptoms, put me at ease
A simple blood test showed your disease

Your girlfriend said to wait; she's on the phone
She talked for hours as you sat alone
Anxious to tell her of your promotion
No concern did she show or any notion
Of the look on your face with such emotion
The job would transfer you out of state
And you wondered if she would wait
You would be gone at least a year
In choosing not to interfere

You took a taxi back home instead
Her line still busy, you went to bed

A church member called up her pastor
To share with him a sad disaster
She heard him sigh so she talked faster
He interjected right away a list
Of things to do but truly missed
The reason she had called him in the first place
He did most of the talking as tears rolled down her face
She felt unimportant and hurt by what he had said
Leaving her with greater pain; now her hope was dead
She opened her Bible to written words in red
A tear fell right on St. Matthew 5:4
For *love* listened, and she wept no more
With a bright smile, she lifted her face
To the Master of Listening Grace
Mercy sat beside her the whole night through
As she poured out the words she *needed* too

No matter if they're young or old
Love hears what is being told
In any hour or any place
Spirit holds us in holy embrace

Who Will You Follow?

Does your soul thirst for fellowship with others in love
Who worship the Creator of this passion from above?

He created all mankind to love and enjoy
All made with purpose and equal in race
So you cannot judge the color of one's face

I am no better and neither are you
Than another human God created
Have you been racist or even hated
Another for the color of their skin
We are all the same within
Born into this world with God's DNA
Makes us all His children anyway
So don't be quick to judge another
Look upon them as a sister or brother
Teach this love to your daughter and your son
We were made in the image of the Holy One

Don't let the devil control your mind
Hate is evil and will leave you hollow
Which one do you choose to follow?
Sinners are condemned and lost
No use for God has a great cost
It will lead you to your doom
Hating gives love no room
To bear fruit of the spirit
Reject evil, don't get near it
Give not your power or your thought
Don't give in I ask you not
To the devil or evil sinner
Be wise in love, the winner

Protected under God's care
He will always be there

Satan will keep you from the light
Kept in darkness and believing his lies
So desensitized to others cries
He delights in your sin an evil way
Pushing you back, he leads you astray
You'll not succeed in a life of hate
Follow pure love before it's too late
Will ignorance make you wait?
Don't be stubborn in your sin
You won't find joy; you'll never win
God keeps His promises to you
You'll find a life you never knew
If you follow the God of love so true

I hope you'll wish to be much more
Purpose filled no longer hollow
And choose the only God you need to follow

Why We Suffer

God in His wisdom had a plan
Many do not understand
Why we lose a child or mother
A dear friend, sister, or brother
Death is a part of human life
And we ask, "Why all our strife?"
With diseases and no cure found
Our loved ones placed on the ground
Too soon or by traumatic event
All our hopes are truly spent
And we ask, "Why all the strife?"
What about the widowed wife
Who cries herself to sleep each night?
A baby born with aids to fight
Is helpless and dies on a dirt floor
Why must we suffer anymore?
God is the Creator of all things
Sometimes suffering He brings
He causes what may not seem right
But has a plan to bring to light
A better you; a purpose willed
Stronger and more fulfilled
Faith is a test we need always
It builds our future days
To change what needed to be
In your will, you did not see

Our bodies are human and will decay
The Perfect One planned it that way
He is supernatural with a pure soul
We are of dust and are not whole

All were sent to earth for a reason
Some chosen for only a season
He knows that child stillborn
That left you so forlorn
Alive in His arms to stay
God's will is the only way
You'll find the truth someday
We must trust His wisdom still
Your happiness won't come until
You reach the understanding; clear
God did not give you a spirit of fear
He knows you and why you're here
Experiences will take us places
Guiding us to unknown faces
Witnessing to them, then and there
What you went through, unaware
They also did but felt alone
In shared sorrows, you've grown
God plants us where we need to be
Not always will we want to see
The suffering we all go through
He waits to see what we will do

He'll never leave your side
And you could never hide
You may not listen to His voice
Sometimes not given a choice
He grabs you gently with love
Revealing your questions of
An answer only you could find
By leaving your own will behind

Don't think He does not care
He's truly always there
The Creator of love and glory
Is the Author of your life story

Many clench their fists in the air
And ask why God was not there
When those they lost and loved so much
Had left their lives and human touch
But God told us at our birth
We're only travelers on this earth
We belong to Him and no other
Not even our father or mother
That's why we cried on our birthing day
Because His arms sent us away
To live a purpose; fruit to bare
Knowing we'd have suffering there

His hand of love is constant on you
So in love with us all, it is true
Suffering carves joy we never knew
Unmasked by faith you did not let go
Reveals His pure love you'll come to know
Why we suffer is in the name of love
To become what we're intended of
One day, He will call my name
I will be whole, never the same
My suffering will be no more
Running through heaven's door
I'll understand my earth life's story
And touch the face of love and glory

Why?

I was burdened by the past
From what I did and said
Then Jesus asked me why
Why do you hurt and cry?

I forgave you long ago
For your heart, I know so well
Don't worry one more day
But continue to pray

Pray for those who judge you
That do not know your heart
They'll never find perfection
In their own reflection

So forgive those who still judge
Or against you; hold a grudge
You are a precious child of God
Created by Him and for Him
You're forgiven; it's true
The cross was carried for you

Wisdom

The pursuit of wisdom brings security
Love knowledge and choose to fear the Lord
When wisdom enters your heart; blessed you will be

She lifts her voice in the square
To deliver you from the evil way
It is life to your soul when she is there
She is more precious than jewels
Nothing else you desire can compare

She is a shield to those who seek her diligently
For your foot will not stumble
You will walk in your way securely
Incline your heart to understanding
Do not be wise in your own eyes
For the Lord will be your confidence
Fools hate knowledge, wisdom they despise
To leave the path of uprightness
Is to walk in the ways of darkness

When wisdom stretches out her hand
Take hold and find heavenly treasure
For its profit is better than silver
Its gain than fine gold, in any measure
She is healing to the body
Refreshment to the bone
Seek her in everything
Her integrity; make your own

She is s tree of life
To those who take hold of her fast

You will find favor and good repute
For peace is added to you at last

Wisdom will guard you
You'll be honored in her embrace
Take hold of her instruction
She'll give you a garland of grace
To wear upon your head
And present you with a crown of beauty
She'll guide your path
And light the way for you to see

To receive her is a wise behavior
Granted by our Holy Savior
Through wisdom we find favor

You

Each day you bring me gifts
I can unwrap with my eyes
Presents from my Father
Like diamonds cut for me
Handcrafted and set in velvet skies

Before the morning light
I awaken to Your love song
Soft and low; doves serenade
Another day for me You made

A gentle breeze weaves through the window
Sweet whispers kiss my ears awake
Refreshed by the breath of You
The greatest love I ever knew

My first love; the first voice I heard
Before You sent me to my mother's womb
When I was born, I heard Your voice again
That was the reason I cried my first cry
I remembered my first love; that is why

You told me I belonged to You
I was Your great miracle
You granted me spirit gifts
Before I could speak a word
Now His first vice is heard

When I am disquieted, You shine Your light
Your peace quilt blankets me warm and calm
Held in Your everlasting arms so gently
I am cradled into sweet tranquility

Every day, You send bouquets
In so many various ways
Through people, hard times, and nature
Spirit weaves through; a gentle purr
Like a child humming, "Amazing Grace"
Spirit-filled contentment lights up your face

You're My Song

I want you to always remember
That I am not far from where you are
I'm closer than an evening star

So dry your tears and laugh for me
Your smiling face I love to see

I hear your laughter in my soul
I'm supernaturally whole
Surrounded by great peace and love
Like an eagle soaring above
I watch over you, my dear
And I am waiting right here
In heaven, yet by your side there
Just whisper my name like a prayer
I will sit with you for a while
And brush my hand across your smile

Be hopeful and please be strong
I still love you; you're my song
We shared so much as man and wife
God blessed us with a happy life

About the Author

Compiling this manuscript, Tricia Banks shed tears. She was humbled as she was led by the Spirit. Although she began writing as a child, she didn't share her poetry until adulthood. She played with angels as a little girl. There were times they had to protect her and guide her. She lives in Waukee, Iowa, and loves it there. Tricia is a blessed mother of seven children, with nineteen grandchildren and seven great-grandchildren.

CPSIA information can be obtained
at www.ICGtesting.com
Printed in the USA
BVHW080038120123
656051BV00001B/53